Nov 22 2019

Dear Judy

May your expanded journey in Judaism bring more interactions with your psychological & spiritual insights. There's a harmony and a fluidity in the fields of religion & psych and I hope they reveal themselves to you in your full life journey.

Shalom, Shalom

Dana Lev

Praise for *Positive Judaism*

"Brings stories, concepts, and research to life to help you make the most of your Judaism. This is an important contribution to how religion can be viewed in a positive way, through the lens of strength, positivity, and well-being. This book may transform the way that you look at and experience Judaism and, more importantly, transform your own well-being and how you bring your inherent virtues forward to help others and improve the world."

—Ryan M. Niemiec, PsyD, education director, VIA Institute on Character, co-author of *The Power of Character Strengths: Appreciate and Ignite Your Positive Personality*

"*Positive Judaism* is the first book of its kind to seamlessly marry the science of well-being with the wisdom of Judaism. Whether you're familiar with Jewish philosophy and new to positive psychology, or vice versa, this book will empower and inspire you with a deep connection to both. Rabbi Darren Levine masterfully weaves research, story, and Jewish principles, giving you practical tools for each of life's stages. This book is a must-read for anyone actively involved in Jewish life, and will serve as a roadmap for helping yourself and others flourish."

—Emiliya Zhivotovskaya, MAPP, MCC, CEO, and founder of the Flourishing Center

"A masterful application of the growing discipline of positive psychology to contemporary Jewish living. Rabbi Levine's own contagious optimism leaps off the pages of this volume. *Positive Judaism* is a marvelous resource for navigating the vicissitudes of life with resilience, hope, and vision. Those who read Rabbi Levine's teachings will discover exciting new pathways to meaning, purpose, and joy."

—Rabbi Ken Chasen, Leo Baeck Temple, Los Angeles, California

"One of my greatest joys over the past decade has been my friendship with Rabbi Darren Levine and the close relationship between our church and his synagogue. And what I've seen is that the principles within this book are not mere theory for him—they are his way of life. His personal embodiment of Positive Judaism has been contagious, transforming not only my own life and the lives of the members of his congregation, but also the culture of downtown New York City as a whole."

—Ryan Holladay, lead pastor of Lower Manhattan Community Church

"Rabbi Darren Levine has given us a much-needed gift for anyone who feels over-worked, stretched too thin, and confused about how to navigate the seemingly limitless set of choices our modern technological world throws at us. *Positive Judaism* is a dazzling blend of insights from the field of positive psychology and inspirational reflections on the ways that Judaism can to help us build richer, happier, and more meaningful lives."

—**Rabbi Mike Uram, author of *Next Generation Judaism: How College Students and Hillel Can Help Reinvent Jewish Organizations*, winner of the 2016 National Jewish Book Award**

"Rabbi Darren Levine puts forward the tenets of a new platform that harmonizes key findings in contemporary social science with long-standing Jewish practices and virtues to create a pathway to authentic happiness. Holding beauty and goodness alongside pain, he combines stories, case studies, and Jewish traditions to suggest how modern Jews can thrive and find meaning in the face of suffering."

—**Rabbi Deborah Waxman, PhD, president, Reconstructing Judaism**

"Anyone seeking a life of achievement, happiness, and total well-being should read this book. It's more than just a guide to your best self. *Positive Judaism* is a systematic way to thriving and flourishing in the world based in Jewish living. Every athlete I know and have known would do well to adopt the principles of Positive Judaism to accomplish great things on and off the court."

—**Jeff Bukantz, president, Maccabi USA Sports for Israel and US Olympic Fencing Team captain, 2004 and 2008**

"Darren Levine offers us a simultaneously scientific and spiritual antidote to the woes of our day. His writing is accessible, practical, and uplifting. He doesn't offer magic or fantasy, but depth of purpose and meaning that teaches that the right balance of Jewish spirituality and substantive psychology can move the dial in our search for purpose and fulfillment. Thank you, Rabbi Levine, for teaching us and leading us to live a life of deeper and more sustainable joy. Bravo!"

—**Rabbi Matthew D. Gewirtz, Congregation B'nai Jeshurun, Short Hills, New Jersey**

"Opening up with his own vulnerability, Rabbi Levine invites us to join him on his exploration of what positive psychology, as seen through Judaism, has to offer the modern condition. Rabbi Levine seamlessly knits together modern science and his successful career in the pulpit to offer us a guidebook to understand Jewish living. This book is a gift to Jews looking to reconnect to a redemptive and positive practice of Judaism."

—**Rabbi Avi Katz Orlow, vice president of innovation and Jewish education, Foundation for Jewish Camp**

"In this wonderful book Rabbi Darren Levine encourages and coaches us to draw from the wellspring of rabbinic and other texts and stories with an urgent invitation to anchor our lives with virtue, optimism, and loving-kindness. *Positive Judaism* accompanies us on our journey to personal and communal wholeness even in moments of challenge and sorrow. I recommend this wonderful life guide to well-being and happiness."

—Rabbi Peter J. Rubinstein, Central Synagogue, New York City, and director of Jewish Community and Bronfman Center for Jewish Life, 92nd Street Y

"More than just a catchy phrase or a passing fad, *Positive Judaism* offers a vision and a possibility for a powerful and relevant Judaism and Jewish experience. Rabbi Levine offers a concise, accessible, and often personal entry point for an emergent understanding of what could possibly unlock the gates of Jewish life for many Jews around the world today and in the future."

—David Bryfman, PhD, CEO, Jewish Education Project

"As I read Rabbi Darren Levine's book, I felt its connections to Seligman's *Authentic Happiness* and Peterson's *Positive Psychology*, as well as echoes of inspiration like that of Marturano's *Finding the Space to Lead*. But it was Gladwell's *The Tipping Point* that came to mind as I sat back and reflected on Rabbi's Levine's statement with this effort. We are at a critical point within the Jewish community in trying to create means of fulfillment and a sense of purpose that can bring us together and closer to our faith in God, in Judaism, in each other, and in humanity. My belief is that *Positive Judaism* will contribute to the tipping point between our search for this and our realization of a better future for ourselves and our communities."

—Aaron Selkow, executive director, URJ Camp Harlam

"Rabbi Levine artfully weaves together the ancient wisdom of Judaism with the modern science of psychology. He offers us a new "guide for the perplexed," illuminating the ways in which Jewish values and practices can guide us in leading a life of well-being and happiness. A book for all those who at some time have wrestled with their connection to religion and their own life journey or who are teaching those that struggle and seek. In other words, all of us."

—Dr. Bill Robinson, dean of the William Davidson Graduate School of Jewish Education of the Jewish Theological Seminary

"In these pages Rabbi Levine teaches us how Jewish values and tradition can guide us to fulfilling relationships, physical and mental health, strong community connections, meaningful work, and purposeful use of wealth. In short, this book can help us live the life we all seek."

—Rabbi Michael S. Friedman, Temple Israel, Westport, Connecticut

"Inspiring and highly relevant to the reader of the twenty-first century. While honestly acknowledging the painful challenges that can be part of life, this book offers real-life strategies to achieve deep spiritual wholeness and happiness."

—Rabbi Mari Chernow, Temple Chai of Phoenix

"An inspiring and wise book. It will lift your spirits and the horizons of Jewish possibility. Rabbi Levine has given a great gift to all of us seeking a life of meaning, depth, and joy."

—Rabbi Evan Moffic, Congregation Solel, Chicago, author of *The Happiness Prayer*

POSITIVE JUDAISM

For a Life of
Well-Being and
Happiness

Rabbi Darren Levine, DMin

BEHRMAN HOUSE

Editor: Kathleen Bloomfield
Project manager/editor: Dena Neusner
Design: Neustudio, Inc.
Copyright © 2019 by Darren Levine
All rights reserved.
Published by Behrman House, Inc.
Millburn, NJ 07041
www.behrmanhouse.com

Please see page 182 for permissions.

ISBN 978-0-87441-999-3
Printed in the United States of America

Library of Congress Cataloging-in-Publication Data
Names: Levine, Darren, Rabbi, author.
Title: Positive Judaism : for a life of well-being and happiness / Rabbi
Darren Levine, D.Min.
Description: Millburn : Behrman House, 2019. | Includes bibliographical
references. | Summary: "How can we increase happiness and well-being in
our lives, using modern science and ancient wisdom? Psychology teaches
us that positive emotions and character traits promote happiness, health,
and well-being. Jewish wisdom and practice have long taught the merits
of optimism and resilience. Positive Judaism combines these powerful
understandings into a practical and spiritual approach to increasing
well-being for ourselves and our communities. In Positive Judaism, you
will find: proven activities to deepen your relationships, practices for
personal transformation in the face of challenges, character strengths
that build physical and mental health. We have so many challenges and
opportunities for growth in our daily lives. The good news is that we have
the tools, both ancient and modern, to guide our way. This is Positive
Judaism."-- Provided by publisher.
Identifiers: LCCN 2019028710 [print] | LCCN 2019028711 [ebook] | ISBN
9780874419993 [hardcover] | ISBN 9781681150536 [ebook]
Subjects: LCSH: Joy--Religious aspects--Judaism. | Happiness--Religious
aspects--Judaism. | Well-being--Religious aspects--Judaism.
Classification: LCC BM645.J67 L48 2019 [print] | LCC BM645.J67 [ebook] |
DDC 296.7--dc23
LC record available at https://lccn.loc.gov/2019028710
LC ebook record available at https://lccn.loc.gov/2019028711

To my parents

Contents

Preface:
How Positive Judaism Was Born

Following my first sermon on Positive Judaism, a woman approached me and said, "Rabbi, my name is Rose. I have been a psychologist for forty-five years. I am the child of Holocaust survivors. I do not believe in God and I'm not an expert in Jewish history, but I can tell you one thing: there is nothing positive about Judaism. With all the anti-Semitism, the problems in Israel, and the guilt, Judaism and positivity simply cannot coexist."

Rose is not alone. I'd heard this narrative before. But I have a different narrative. For me, Judaism offers a richness, a joy, a comfort. With its focus on family, community, social justice, education, and customs, Judaism has always been a positive force in my life. But then one day, quite unexpectedly, Judaism took on a new level of significance for me.

It was a wintry Thursday in New York City. A member of my synagogue called to ask if I could visit her critically ill, six-year-old son in the hospital. I cleared my schedule, put a gift bag together, and jumped into a taxi.

As the taxi crossed the intersection at East Thirtieth Street and Second Avenue, I instinctively looked to my left. A delivery truck had missed a red light and was barreling toward us. I braced for impact.

When I came to, I was in an ambulance with the sirens wailing and paramedics hovering over me. No longer was I on my way to the hospital as a visitor; I was now an accident victim.

In the hospital, images of my life filled my thoughts: my childhood, my friends, my travels, my colleagues, and my children. The nurses may have thought I was crying from the pain, but they were tears of appreciation, joy, and a clarity that I had never felt before. Like Jonah in the belly of the whale, I was experiencing a wake-up call of biblical proportions. A rebirth.

At some point that afternoon, my inner voice said, "Darren, this was not your day to die. You have been blessed with a second chance. Don't be unhappy."

The truth was, I was unhappy. Despite my love for my family and a professional life focused on supporting families, my own marriage was in shambles. Although I was putting on the best show I could for my children, my extended family, and my congregation, I was hurting.

After many hours of medical tests and examinations, my doctor reported that I was very lucky. Aside from bruises and cuts, I was fine, and I could leave.

As I approached the exit, I heard someone call my name. A nurse was coming toward me with a bag—the gift I had brought for my congregant's son. Immediately, my mind flashed to the Jewish teaching that when one is on a mission to deliver goodness to someone else, the Divine One protects their journey.

With humility, I turned back to fulfill the original purpose of my visit. When I came to the child's room, his mother was sitting at his bedside.

"I thought a little gift might cheer you up," I said and gave the gift bag to the boy.

"Thank you, Rabbi," said his mother.

"Thank you" was all I could say. *Thank you.*

• • •

On my way home that night, I imagined some of the changes that were ahead in my life. A highly emotional day like this may have brought a loving couple closer together. But the events of that day had the opposite effect on my wife and me. We both knew the marriage was over. We talked. We cried. We separated that night.

I was all over the place emotionally, but I felt so alive. As I tried to steel my nerves, a book on the shelf caught my attention, *Authentic Happiness: Using the New Positive Psychology to Realize Your Potential for Lasting Fulfillment* by Martin Seligman. Exactly what I needed: happiness, positivity, and fulfillment.

I read the book cover to cover. The ideas of positive psychology spoke to me on a deeply personal level. They felt natural. Resilience, optimism, hope, bravery, perseverance, spirituality, awe, love, meditation, self-awareness, and courage—the ingredients of authentic happiness.

Months later, I felt ready to share my personal story of the accident, marital separation, and recovery. I chose a Friday evening Shabbat service and spoke about the elements that helped me piece my life back together: the friendships and community that supported me; the love of and for my children; my desire to continue my rabbinic work; the inner strengths, like optimism, resilience, and hope, that held me together. The accident had been an awakening.

And that night, it hit me.

The virtues of authentic happiness had already been living inside me but in a different language. They were in my Jewish heart and mind and had been growing in me since childhood. To explain this flash of insight, I said, "This is Positive Judaism."

That was the same night Rose approached to say that "Judaism and positivity simply cannot coexist."

This book is for Rose and for anyone seeking to understand how Judaism can provide them with a life of authentic happiness and why this approach to life and religion is more important in our world today than ever before.

"First a person should put his own
house together, then his town,
and then the world. In other words,
first his own well-being, then his
community's well-being, and then
the well-being of the world."
—Rabbi Israel Salanter (1809–1883)

Introduction:
A New Vision for Jewish Life in the Twenty-First Century

We're living during a complex time in history. Social and technological progress has raised the quality of life across the globe, yet at the same time, the rates of depression, suicide, drug abuse, obesity, divorce, and loneliness have reportedly reached epic proportions.[1] And while participation in faith communities may have been an antidote for some of these issues in previous generations, membership at most synagogues and churches is shrinking.[2] Either people no longer see the positive value that faith communities can bring to their lives, or faith organizations are pointed in the wrong direction.

This book is meant to shift this trend. It pairs ancient Jewish wisdom with modern well-being theory to help individuals and families improve their lives and, simultaneously, elevate the mission of sacred communities to become thriving and flourishing social centers.

The good news is that we have the tools, both ancient and modern, to guide our way.

First, the ancient way. We tell stories. Wisdom and tradition have been passed down from generation to generation through storytelling. For example:

There once lived a man named Azyk. One night, Azyk dreamed of a great treasure hidden under a bridge in Warsaw. He woke up early the next morning and decided he needed to find this treasure, and so he set off. When he arrived at the bridge, he sought the exact spot he dreamed of the night before, but there was a guard standing there.

Azyk paced back and forth all day long, but the guard never

moved. Finally, the guard approached him and said, "What are you doing here?" Azyk told him the truth. "I came to the bridge because I dreamed of treasure here." Replied the guard, "That's funny, I too dreamed of a treasure last night that was hidden under the kitchen stove of a house that belonged to a man named Azyk."

Astonished, Azyk turned around and went home. Sure enough, when he dug under his stove, he found a great treasure and became a very rich man.

This story demonstrates that we often look far afield for the things we value most. However, if we look hard enough, we can often find this treasure close to home. The treasure I am referring to is authentic happiness. As we explore Positive Judaism together, we will draw upon the richness of Jewish teachings, practices, and rituals that lead to a life of happiness and well-being.

Well-being in Judaism is best translated as *r'vachah nafshit*, representing the constructs of life satisfaction, thriving, flourishing, and meaning—all describing a distinct yet related experience of the good life. Related to well-being is happiness, *osher* in Hebrew, which describes positive emotions like joy, pleasure, and comfort. Well-being and happiness, *r'vachah nafshit v'osher*, this is the ancient language.

In the twenty-first century, in addition to the ancient ways, we can also draw upon modern tools like data and research to guide our way to well-being and happiness. Today, we embrace the scientific method, and research studies on human advancement help us to better understand ways to thrive and to flourish.

Bookstore shelves are full of books on happiness. University courses on happiness are fast becoming the most popular classes online and on campuses where they are offered.[3] Health care agencies like CIGNA run large-scale studies on factors that lead to well-being, and governments like the United States and Bhutan are measuring the level of Gross National Happiness (GNH).[4] The United Nations has even declared March 20 to be the International Day of Happiness.[5]

People, organizations, and governments want to know the facts. Yet, contrary to what many people believe, happiness has little to do with where people live, their income, their material possessions, or their popularity. It's something every person must discover for themselves by looking inward, not outward. Like our story of Azyk, happiness is often found close to home. Whether or not it is under your kitchen floor today, the research suggests that, as it is for Azyk, happiness is something you can discover for yourself, for your family, and for your community, by learning the tools for well-being.

• • •

This guidebook is organized into four parts. Part One lays out the platform for Positive Judaism and the basic theory of happiness and well-being. We will explore three frameworks for well-being, character strengths, and positivity. This will be followed by a review of research showing the reasons why religious people rank above average in measures of happiness and well-being.

With the modern language of well-being established, we'll turn to the principles of Positive Judaism. Next, we introduce the ten Jewish happiness virtues and the ten Jewish well-being practices that extend Positive Judaism into daily life.

Part Two illustrates how Positive Judaism can be applied to the most important areas of life: relationships, health, community, work, and money. These five areas serve as the framework of this book, because prior research has demonstrated they are where people spend most of their time and energy. Learning to improve the quality of our experiences in each of these areas opens opportunities to increase the meaning, happiness, and well-being in our lives and in the lives of those around us.

Part Three examines the flip side of these five areas of life. Life is not always easy, nor do people always feel positive. There is suffering and sorrow along the journey. There are broken relationships, illness, loneliness, job loss, and financial problems. Fortunately, there are specific Jewish virtues and practices to help individuals pass through disappointments, trauma, and losses on the pathway to well-being.

Part Four includes a series of letters written to encourage the growth of happiness and well-being in the lives of individuals, communities, and ultimately, the world. The teachings in this book can go beyond Judaism to have a broad application in religious and spiritual living. I imagine a "Positive Religion" focused on well-being, positivity, and happiness to improve humanity and the world. All people, no matter their backgrounds, can apply these principles of well-being in a religious context to create a more compassionate and kinder world. That is the hope of this book, and I believe it to be the great hope of Judaism.

Part One

Ancient Wisdom, Modern Science

Positive Judaism is the pairing of ancient wisdom and modern science to help raise well-being in the lives of individuals, communities, and the world. But what exactly is well-being, and how do we gain more of it? Tom Rath and Jim Harter, senior scientists at Gallup International, studied hundreds of thousands of people in over 130 countries to explore the following question: Are there contributors to well-being that transcend nationality, race, age, and religion?

They concluded that, regardless of geographic location, well-being results from how people experience five key areas in their lives: relationships, health, community, work, and money.[6]

In Part One, we will:

- Link Jewish wisdom to the five key areas of life.
- Define well-being and happiness, and explain the emotional and physical benefits of living to flourish and thrive.
- Present a Jewish perspective on three scientific theories of well-being—PERMA, VIA classification of character strengths and virtues, and broaden-and-build—and explore how positivity can be increased by living a Jewish life.
- Present the principles of Positive Judaism and introduce ten Jewish happiness virtues and ten Jewish

well-being practices that will inform each chapter
going forward.

The theories and principles we introduce in Part One will provide the
grounding for an exploration of the many ways Positive Judaism can
elevate our lives. Let's journey now into the ideas and research that
support this approach to faith and religion.

1

"Happy shall you be, and it shall be good for you."
—PSALM 128:2

The Science of Well-Being and Happiness

A person approached Rabbi Hillel in the second century and asked, "Can you teach me the entire Torah while I stand on one foot?" Hillel replied, "What is hateful to you, do not do to your neighbor. That is the whole Torah."[7]

If I were asked a similar question today in the twenty-first century, "Can you teach the purpose of Judaism while standing on one foot?" I would offer the text from the Book of Psalms above and add, "Seek happiness and well-being for you and your neighbor. That is the whole purpose of Judaism."

The happiness I'm imagining is not fleeting or selfish pleasure, but rather a profound state of wholeness, a deep sense of well-being. Aristotle said, "Happiness [*eudaimonia*] is the meaning and purpose of life, the ultimate goal."[8] In other words, happiness comes from living a life of virtue, pursuing wisdom, and living up to our destiny and best life possible.

In Pursuit of Happiness

Many people are struggling to find happiness in their lives. Some may be burdened with illness, loneliness, or financial stress. Others may be suffering physically, emotionally, or mentally. Some may be very poor, while others may have material comforts, a busy social life, relatively good health, yet still feel unsettled and unhappy. Regardless of the reasons why, many people are struggling to imagine a life of authentic happiness and well-being.

We can benefit in the twenty-first century from a new science of well-being that aims to help people find greater happiness in their lives. For too long, people thought that well-being meant the absence of suffering, and our health-care industry created interventions, like medications and treatments, designed to relieve suffering. But helping people to not suffer does not equate with helping people to live well. The skills people need to live well and that families need to thrive are different from the skills needed to address suffering and unhappiness.

There are many pathways to living well, and the new science of well-being has several theories that support a flourishing and thriving life. Each is designed to help people elevate their lives and improve their well-being and happiness. We are going to explore three of them in this book and show how they pair organically with Jewish life and wisdom.

Jacob's Ladder: Climbing Higher to Well-Being

In the Bible, the story of Jacob's ladder presents a good image for the pursuit of well-being:

> Jacob left Beer-Sheba and set out for Haran. He came upon a certain place and stopped there for the night, for the sun had set. Taking one of the stones of that place, he put it under his head and lay down in that place. He had a dream; a [ladder] was set on the ground and its top reached to the sky, and angels of God were going up and down on it. And the [Eternal One] was standing beside him and [God] said: "I am the [Eternal,] the God of your father Abraham and the God of Isaac: the ground on which you are lying I will assign to you and to your offspring. Your descendants shall be as the dust of the earth; you shall spread out to the west and to the east, to the north and to the south. All the families of the earth shall bless themselves by you and your descendants. Remember, I am with you: I will protect you wher-

ever you go and will bring you back to this land. I will not leave you until I have done what I have promised you."

Jacob woke from his sleep and said, "Surely God is present in this place, and I did not know it!" Shaken, he said, "How awesome is this place! This is none other than the abode of God, and that is the gateway to heaven."[9]

Some could imagine this ladder as an apt metaphor for the ups and downs in the pursuit of well-being. Up the rungs when we feel happy, down the rungs when we feel sad. But what if authentic happiness was imagined differently? What if we imagined the rungs as stages toward well-being and that our life was continually forward moving, even when we faced challenges and disappointments like hard stones under our heads? As if we could wake up from our sleep with a new perspective and say, "How awesome is this place! This is none other than a life of happiness and well-being, and this is the gateway to heaven."

To arrive at this new perspective, we must imagine that our goal in life is beyond basic functioning. People want to thrive, not just survive, which is rooted in the Psalmist's assurance, "Happy shall you be, and it shall be good for you."[10]

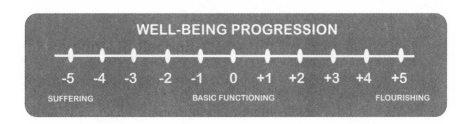

We can explore this idea on a horizontal ladder, like the one pictured here. The zero point represents a person's basic functioning. The previous goal was to move people along the ladder from suffering to basic functioning, and that was considered success.

Yet what if the project of well-being could be expanded far beyond suffering? How could a new approach to life help people climb beyond basic functioning and ascend toward a flourishing life? Moreover, what if, no matter where one started on the progression, there was always the potential to increase well-being, health, and happiness?

Thanks to recent developments in the science of well-being, these questions are being answered. The result is a new paradigm that seeks to move people beyond basic functioning toward flourishing. While each person, family, and community will climb the rungs to happiness in their own unique way, the latest research suggests that to progress in well-being, people should focus on increasing their positive thoughts, emotions, and behavior in five key areas of life: relationships, health, community, work, and money.

The Five Areas of Well-Being

The five areas of well-being differentiate a thriving life from one consumed with suffering and challenges.[11] Overall happiness can improve, with focus and attention in the following five areas, as summarized by Rath and Harter:[12]

- **Relationships:** People with relationship well-being are surrounded by people who encourage their development and growth, accept them for who they are, and treat them with respect. They deliberately spend time investing in the networks that surround them.

- **Health:** People with good health manage their health well. They exercise regularly, and as a result, they feel better. They make good dietary choices, which keeps their energy high throughout the day and sharpens their thinking. They get enough sleep to process what they have learned the day before and to get a good start on the next day.

- **Community:** People with high community well-being feel safe and secure where they live and participate in their local community. They take pride in their community and feel that it is headed in the right direction. This often results in their wanting to give back and make a lasting contribution to society.

- **Work:** People with high work well-being wake up every morning with something to look forward to doing each day. They do work that fits their strengths and interests. They have a deep purpose in life and a plan to attain their goals. In most cases, they have a leader who motivates them and makes them enthusiastic about the future.

- **Money:** People with high financial well-being manage their personal finances well and spend their money wisely. They buy experiences instead of just material possessions, and they give to others instead of always spending on themselves. At a basic level, they are satisfied with their overall standard of living.

If the answer to a life of authentic happiness is found in these five areas, the next question is, how do we increase well-being in these five areas? There are many theories that address this question, and we will explore three of them: PERMA, VIA classification of character strengths and virtues, and broaden-and-build.

Well-Being Theory 1: The PERMA Model

The first well-being theory is called PERMA, an acronym for "Positive emotion, Engagement, Relationships, Meaning, and Accomplishment."

In the summer of 2017, I joined several thought leaders in Uluru, Australia, for a gathering of the Imagination Institute, a special initiative of the Center for Positive Psychology at the University of Pennsylvania. Led by Dr. Martin Seligman, we met for a long weekend of conversations, presentations, and collective brainstorming about the relationship between imagination and spirituality.

One of Dr. Seligman's many contributions to the field of well-being is the PERMA model, a theory of well-being that can measure and help people improve their happiness.[13] Dr. Seligman and his colleagues have found that when people experience **P**ositive emotions, deepen their **E**ngagement with the activities that help them grow, build strong **R**elationships and social connections, live with **M**eaning and reach for greater purpose, and set goals to **A**ccomplish, they report a greater level of life satisfaction and happiness.

- **Positive emotions:** Feeling positive emotion can arise from the way we remember a past event with gratitude or laughter, experience a current moment with joy or savoring, and anticipate a future experience with hope or optimism. Boosting positive emotion and joy leads to increased happiness.

- **Engagement:** To be engaged is to enter a flow state, sometimes referred to as "being in the zone," where we are absorbed in an experience that uses our skills, strengths, and attention, where self-awareness disappears, where the

perception of time stops, and where the activity is its own reward. Flow can be experienced in many ways, and examples could include dancing, praying, lovemaking, playing a musical instrument, and physical exercise. Greater engagement in a state of flow leads to increased happiness.

• **Relationships:** To be in relationship is to have connections to others that offer support and a sense of belonging in the world. Developing strong relationships is important for nourishing the qualities of love, compassion, kindness, cooperation, and empathy. Higher-quality relationships with friends, family, colleagues, and humanity lead to increased happiness.

• **Meaning:** To have meaning is to belong and to serve something bigger than oneself, by attaching to institutions like family, schools, religion, social justice, work organizations, politics, and so on. Increased happiness comes from serving a larger purpose in life, which confers meaning.

• **Accomplishment:** To accomplish is to achieve and be competent and successful in a variety of areas including the workplace, athletics, hobbies, family, and so on. To accomplish goals and to be successful in tasks lead to increased happiness.

Judaism is a living experience of PERMA. As a congregational rabbi, I witness people experiencing positive emotions at Shabbat and holiday gatherings where there is joy and uplift. People are engaged in community and something larger than their individual lives. **R**elationships are essential, and one of the main drivers of any congregation is to bring people together in meaningful exchanges to accomplish greater good for humanity. While every religious community gathers differently, the most positive ones are living experiences of PERMA.

In addition, studies show that religiously identified people report that they are happier and more satisfied with life than those who have no ties to religion.[14] It's here, in the religious context, where people can best express their most human values like optimism, kindness, and gratitude. In the best cases, it's also in a religious setting where people learn to appreciate and develop certain psychological strengths like bravery, courage, authenticity, love of learning, humility, and forgiveness. The latest research concludes the following:

- Religious people report higher levels of happiness and health and recover better after trauma.[15]

- The social support, fellowship, and sense of identity within a religious community help people to feel less isolated and able to share in one another's burdens as well as accomplishments.[16]

- The strong emotional experiences of worship and prayer provide comfort and encourage awe, wonder, and a search for the Divine.[17]

- Faith education provides the context to ask existential questions: Who am I? What is my life for? Where do I fit in? Who is the Creator? How do I live a virtuous life and improve the world around me?

Jewish living activates all the elements of PERMA and, in the best settings, develops and deepens PERMA, guiding people forward on their ladder of well-being. To gain a better understanding of the level of well-being in your life today, I invite you to take the PERMA Well-Being Profiler in appendix A.

Well-Being Theory 2: The VIA Classification of Character Strengths and Virtues

A second scientific theory of well-being focuses on the development of character strengths. Dr. Lea Waters, director of the Centre for Positive Psychology at the University of Melbourne, defines character strengths as positive qualities that we perform well, that we choose often, and that energize us. Strengths are personal qualities that are used in productive ways to contribute to our goals and growth. They are built and developed over time through our innate ability and dedicated effort. These qualities are recognized by others as praiseworthy. Overall, they contribute positively to the lives of others.[18]

The VIA Institute on Character, led by Dr. Neal Mayerson and Dr. Ryan Niemiec, identifies twenty-four character strengths that fall under six categories: wisdom, courage, humanity, justice, temperance, and transcendence.[19]

VIA Classification of Character Strengths and Virtues

Traits	Definitions, Characteristics, and Strengths
Wisdom	Cognitive strengths that support acquiring and utilizing knowledge: **perspective, curiosity, creativity, love of learning,** and **judgment**
Courage	Emotional strengths that develop the willpower to achieve goals in the face of internal or external opposition: **bravery, perseverance, honesty,** and **resilience**
Humanity	Interpersonal strengths that develop authentic human connections and friendship: **love, kindness,** and **social intelligence**
Justice	Civic strengths that support connections to community: **teamwork, fairness,** and **leadership**
Temperance	Relational strengths that develop sufficiency and wholeness: **forgiveness, humility, prudence,** and **self-regulation**
Transcendence	Metaphysical strengths that develop existential meaning: **appreciation of beauty, gratitude, hope, humor,** and **spirituality**

Everyone has *signature strengths*, the top five strengths that come most naturally to them. When we can identify and activate our signature strengths, we can compensate for those strengths that are less prominent.

Dr. Waters teaches that people of all ages who know their signature strengths, work to develop them every day, and understand how to activate them to overcome their challenges experience these general advantages:[20]

1. Greater levels of happiness at work

2. Better work performance

3. Greater likelihood of staying married and being happy in their marriage

4. Higher levels of physical fitness and healthy behaviors

5. Increased levels of life satisfaction and self-esteem

6. Reduced risk of depression

7. Enhanced ability to cope with stress and adversity

Activating character strengths and knowing our own signature strengths supports well-being by encouraging us to live in our power areas. The Signature Strengths Survey in appendix B will assist you in identifying your character strengths.

I've taken this survey many times, and my top character strengths are ingenuity, curiosity, social intelligence, perspective, and leadership. However, near the bottom of my list is forgiveness. It may seem odd that a rabbi ranks low in forgiveness, but I have a very hard time with this strength. It's not that I cannot, do not, or will not forgive. Forgiveness just does not come as naturally to me as my signature strengths. I've therefore had to learn some forgiveness hacks. When people cross me or act self-centered, I react within my strength areas: curiosity, perspective, and social intelligence. I eventually get to forgiveness, but it usually takes me more time than someone who has forgiveness as a signature strength.

Jewish tradition has identified character strengths, or virtues, that are essential to living a life of values, meaning, and ethics.[21] The rabbinic sages believed that only one who possesses qualities that inspire good deeds can experience the happy life.[22] The Talmud expands on this and teaches that "Torah is learned through forty-eight virtues, known by their Hebrew name, *midot*."[23] By observing and developing these virtues, we strengthen our character.

The famous twelfth-century Jewish physician, philosopher, and scholar Moses Maimonides taught that we must choose to live at our "golden mean," the balanced midpoint between two extreme virtues.[24] Take bravery and cowardice, for example. Too much bravery may put someone in a dangerous situation, whereas too much cowardice may be equally dangerous. We must strive to balance our character strengths and to find our golden mean.

As the Chasidic master Rabbi Meir Chodesh (1898–1989) taught, "It is not the treatment of anger that needs working on, but the truth of goodwill. Once a person's anger is aroused, it is too late to work on it." In other words, as a technique to ascend the ladder of well-being, it is more important to know and develop our strengths than to focus on our weaknesses.

Well-Being Theory 3: The Broaden-and-Build Theory of Positivity

In our third well-being theory, we explore the role that emotions have on our overall state of happiness. Dr. Barbara Fredrickson at the University of North Carolina–Chapel Hill is the expert in emotional research and has created the broaden-and-build model to show that emotions like joy, gratitude, awe, and love support well-being. When we feel these positive emotions, we are open to possibility and to a wider range of thoughts and actions than are typical.[25]

On the other hand, negative emotions, like anger, resentment, fear, or disgust, restrict well-being and happiness because they create fear, anxiety, and stress.[26] So, in the pursuit of well-being, one should seek to expand, broaden, and build positive emotions because embracing positivity creates several gains in life:

- People who experience more positivity in their lives grow psychologically. They become more optimistic, more resilient, more open, more accepting, and more driven by purpose.

- Positivity builds social connections with others and ignites joy in others.[27]

- Positivity predicts lower levels of stress-related hormones like cortisol and higher levels of hormones like oxytocin. Positivity sends a boost of dopamine and enhances immune system functioning.[28]

- Positivity is correlated with desirable health outcomes like lower blood pressure, less pain, fewer colds, and better sleep. Positive people are also less likely to have hypertension, diabetes, or a stroke.

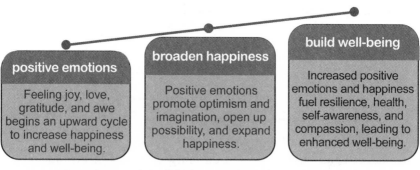

Broaden-and-Build Theory of Positive Emotions

The image above illustrates that positive emotions are not only stand-alone moments in time but can also produce well-being and higher functioning over the long term due to their cumulative effect. Experiencing positive emotions on a regular basis puts people on a trajectory to overall well-being and happiness because each positive emotional experience leads to ideas and activities that build more positive experiences, creating a ripple effect.

I've shared these findings on positivity with Jewish groups, and inevitably someone calls me out. "Rabbi, my *bubbe* [grandmother] raised me on *kvetching*, and she lived to be 120! Never a day went by without her complaints. To me, that's being Jewish." How can I disagree? My late *bubbe* certainly did her share of *kvetching*. But overall, she had a positive soul and a joyful disposition, and my experience and memory of her is love, tenderness, and wisdom.

The ancient rabbis taught a similar lesson to the broaden-and-build theory, which they called *Mitzvah goreret mitzvah*, "One good deed leads to another."[29] For example, when people perform a good deed, like helping someone in need, they will likely feel pride, which boosts positivity. This positive emotion may inspire them to perform more good deeds and to "broaden and build" on their feeling of pride and accomplishment, which will raise their level of well-being. This cycle of goodness elevates the human character and develops more personal resources by creating a feel-good response that inspires people to do more and more good deeds. Doing good deeds is a central practice of living a Jewish life.

Say *L'chayim*—To Life!

One evening, a young boy dropped a coin and was looking for it on the ground when a friend approached.

"What are you doing?" asked the friend.

"I'm looking for a coin I lost."

"Where did you lose it?"

"I lost it way over there."

"Then why are you searching for it here?"

"Because this is where the light is shining," said the boy.

By looking in the right place, we can increase our well-being. Moses Maimonides taught that "every human being may [choose to] become righteous like Moses our Teacher, or wicked like Jeroboam; merciful or cruel, miserly or generous, and so with all other qualities."[30]

In taking stock of the three theories of well-being (PERMA, character strengths, and broaden-and-build) and how to apply them to our lives, there is another factor to consider: our propensity for well-being. Simply put, each person has a different threshold for happiness based on their own unique life.

Take for example, two individuals, Rob and Janet. We should not attempt to compare Rob's well-being to Janet's because both Rob and Janet are completely different people. The goal is not for Rob to aspire to Janet's level of happiness, but rather for both Rob and Janet to aspire to their own individual best lives that only they can imagine for themselves. The same is true for each family and each community.

To best understand the factors that contribute to well-being, we need to know what falls within our control and what factors are outside our influence. Dr. Sonja Lyubomirsky, a professor and positive psychology researcher at the University of California–Riverside, has popularized a model for understanding a person's well-being. There are three factors: genes that we inherit (50 percent), personal circumstances (10 percent), and intentional activities (40 percent).[31]

Circumstances like being married or divorced, renting or owning a home, and living in a city or in the suburbs explain only 10 percent of the variation between people's level of happiness. By the same logic, 50 percent of the differences in people's well-being can be accounted for by genetic factors such as temperament.

The final 40 percent can be directly attributed to our everyday routines, our mind-sets, and our choices. While we cannot change the genes we inherit or our past life experiences, we can change our mind-set and reframe past experiences in a positive way. For example, someone who got fired from a job ten years ago can choose to be angry, bitter, and resentful. Or, the person can choose to think, "Getting fired from that job opened me to new life experiences. I would not be the person I am today without that forced change."

Jewish tradition teaches that we are responsible for our well-being and happiness. In the words of the Talmud, "A person is always liable for [himself], whether awake or asleep."[32] Bottom line: people who are happy and scale high in well-being for themselves choose a lifestyle in which they:[33]

- Devote a great amount of time to family, friends, and community and invest a lot of time nurturing and enjoying those relationships.

- Are comfortable expressing gratitude for all they have.

- Are often the first to offer a helping hand to coworkers.

- Practice optimism when imagining their futures.

- Savor life's pleasures and try to live in the present moment.

- Make physical exercise a regular habit.

- Are deeply committed to lifelong goals and ambitions.

Now we have the theories and the factors that help us understand and contribute to happiness, but it's a choice to make this journey. Reb Tevye sings in *Fiddler on the Roof*, "To life, to life, *l'chayim!*" We are all like Tevye, seeking out happiness for ourselves and our family, facing joys and disappointments. And like Tevye, we have the same task: to find our way to well-being no matter what comes our way, so that before it's too late, we too can sing to the world with authentic happiness, "To life, to life, *l'chayim . . . l'chayim, l'chayim,* to life."

2 "We all live with the objective of being happy;
 our lives are all different yet the same."

—ANNE FRANK

Positive Judaism: Principles, Practices, and Virtues

While Anne Frank's words above are a fitting description of the human condition, how do we grow from having happiness as an objective to actually being happy and living well?

Judaism is not Pollyannaish about the realities of life. It recognizes that real life is not always happy and that we live in the balance between the highs and the lows. We enjoy marriage and endure divorce; we delight in good health and cope with illness; we celebrate birth and mourn death; we relish job success and bear its failure; we appreciate financial riches and temper its ruin.

As "birth is a beginning and death a destination,"[34] how can we make the journey in the best possible way? How can we gain the wisdom to live well at every stage? Is living the good life pure luck, or can we direct the well-lived life with intentionality? It's natural to ask these questions at different turning points, but the answers become clearer at the end of a person's life as one's journey nears the final gate.

The Sacred Journey to Happiness

It is very humbling to sit with people at the end of their life. Some say, "I wish I did things that made me happier." Others share, "I wish I worked less and spent more time with my children." Or, "I wish I traveled more."

Sometimes the confessions are deeper. "I wish that I had married another man, but my mother didn't like him. I never forgave her for that." Or, "Acting was my passion. I loved the stage, and the theater was my home. But my father told me to find a real career. That's what I did. But every day, I resented going to the office." When I hear these regrets, Job's warning in the Bible comes to mind: "My days fly swifter than a runner; they flee without seeing happiness."[35]

Less often do people say, "Rabbi, I lived my life in exactly the way that I wanted to, and now I am ready. It was not always easy. Plenty of hard times. Job losses, some illness, money was tight when my kids were young, and my husband and I had our ups and downs. But looking back, I would not change a day."

At every funeral that I officiate, I read this poem written by the late Rabbi Alvin Fine (1916–1999) because it so beautifully summarizes the arc of life:

> Birth is a beginning,
> And death a destination;
> But life is a journey,
> A going—a growing
> From stage to stage.
>
> From childhood to maturity
> And youth to age.
> From innocence to awareness
> And ignorance to knowing;
> From foolishness to discretion
> And then perhaps wisdom.

From weakness to strength
Or strength to weakness—
And, often, back again.
From health to sickness
And back, we pray, to health again.

From offense to forgiveness,
From loneliness to love,
From joy to gratitude,
From pain to compassion,
And grief to understanding—
From fear to faith.

From defeat to defeat to defeat—
Until, looking backward or ahead,
We see that victory lies
Not at some high place along the way,
But in having made the journey,
Stage by stage—
A sacred pilgrimage.

Birth is a beginning,
And death a destination;
But life is a journey,
A sacred pilgrimage
Made stage by stage—
From birth to death
To life everlasting.[36]

A person is born, and the sacred pilgrimage begins. For however long their journey may be, some people arrive at the final chapter of their lives with contentment, while others arrive with regret. I believe that in normal circumstances, this is determined by how well people experience the five areas of life: relationships, health, community, work, and money. Thus, in order to help people focus on living their best possible life, these five areas serve as the foundation for the principles of Positive Judaism.

The Principles of Positive Judaism

The guiding principles of Positive Judaism are grounded in real life and real-world living for the purpose of raising well-being and happiness for individuals, families, and communities.

One

Positive Judaism asserts that every person is created in the divine image and deserves to live well. The purpose of life is to optimize well-being and happiness for self, family, community, and humanity. This is accomplished by observing holidays and life-cycle traditions, through study and prayer, and by developing personal virtues. This will encourage us to take responsibility for our well-being by drawing on our natural talents and strengths to activate positive emotions, engagement, relationships, meaning, and accomplishment in our life.

Two

Positive Judaism encourages caring, loving, and trusting personal relationships. It's not the number of relationships, it's the quality that matters. People who flourish have friends and family who love, support, and care for them through honest and mutually supportive lifelong relationships. We honor "Love your neighbor as yourself"[37] and Judaism's Golden Rule: "That which is hateful to you, do not do to your fellow; that is the whole Torah, the rest is commentary. Go and learn it."[38]

Three

Positive Judaism encourages strong physical, mental, emotional, and spiritual health. We must be diligent in our health care and invest quality time, effort, and resources into maintaining good physical health and emotional well-being. Daily exercise, good diet, low stress, and quality sleep are essential to well-being. In the words of Maimonides, "Maintaining a healthy and sound body is among the ways of God."[39]

Four

Positive Judaism encourages people to fully participate in supportive faith communities and to connect with *k'lal Yisrael*, the Jewish people, on a local and global level. We need a place to expand our hearts and minds, to celebrate life, to feel the support of others in difficult times, and to provide a spiritual anchor for ourselves and our families. It is in community where Judaism is transmitted from one generation to the next, where we find support at all stages in our life, and where we belong and contribute to something greater than ourselves.

Five

Positive Judaism encourages individuals to pursue work as an expression of their life purpose. We should be diligent about finding our unique life calling. Most people are happiest by doing work that benefits others and simultaneously supports their own financial independence. Communities, schools, and organizations should invest resources to help people of all ages identify a work and career path that offers the greatest sense of accomplishment. To achieve authentic happiness, we must find the life that wants to live in us.

Six

Positive Judaism encourages people to use their money to create well-being.
We should spend money to support our lives, our health, and our community. Money should be earned for the purpose of expanding our well-being and happiness and be spent to become wise through education and culture, to give charity to create a just and fair world, and to create experiences that deepen relationships. The goal of Positive Judaism is not to have more, but to become more.

Seven

Positive Judaism emphasizes human flourishing, life satisfaction, and happiness as the pathway for Jewish continuity. The joy of Judaism and the richness of Jewish tradition cannot survive on negativity. For too long, the narrative in the Jewish community has been about surviving destruction, whether it be the Holocaust, intermarriage, or anti-Semitism. While these are important, there must be more to the Jewish mission in the twenty-first century. Rather than survive, the new purpose must be to guide individuals, families, and communities to thrive.

Similar to the Seven Noachide Laws, which are biblical commands for all the children of Noah (i.e., all humanity) to ensure a righteous life and future, the seven core principles of Positive Judaism are truths for all, with the distinct goal of raising well-being and happiness for all humanity. How these principles are expressed so that people and communities can raise their well-being is the task ahead.

Ten Jewish Happiness Virtues and Ten Jewish Well-Being Practices

In this book, we will focus on ten virtues and ten practices that help activate the experience of Positive Judaism. Virtues are similar to character strengths and personal ethics, whereas practices include rituals and actions. These ideals have been chosen because modern science has demonstrated their value in raising happiness and well-being.

Ten Jewish Happiness Virtues	Ten Jewish Well-Being Practices
Resilience: *ko'ach*	Experience Shabbat
Optimism: *tikvah*	Prayer and Personal Reflection
Loving-kindness: *g'milut chasadim*	Actively Participate in Community
Wisdom: *chochmah*	Learn and Study
Justice: *tzedek*	Give Charity
Forgiveness: *s'lichah*	Observe Yom Kippur and Forgive
Courage: *ometz lev*	Visit the Sick
Spirituality: *ruchni'ut*	The Passover Seder
Gratitude: *hakarat hatov*	Express Gratitude by Volunteering
Perseverance: *hatmada*	Meditation

This is where ancient wisdom meets modern science. The rabbi may see these virtues and practices as ways to grow spiritually and deepen one's connection to Jewish tradition. The psychologist may see these virtues and practices as skills to improve happiness and well-being.

These ten virtues and practices describe an informed pathway to the flourishing life. It is up to each person, family, and community to find their own meaningful and positive way to engage in them. The next chapters will examine these virtues and practices one at a time, but before we move ahead, I want to briefly respond to Rose, who said to me, "There is nothing positive about Judaism."

I have not seen Rose since the night I first mentioned Positive Judaism. However, over the years, I have doubtless thought more about her than she has about me, because Rose represents someone very close to me—myself.

If I ever meet Rose again, I would like to say the following:

I understand that you feel there is nothing positive about Judaism. As a career psychologist and child of Holocaust survivors, there is probably little you have not witnessed in your career and personal life. As a man and a rabbi, I too have seen much pain, suffering, and brokenness in our world. Yet, I have also witnessed abundant beauty, kindness, and so very much love.

Fair or unfair, Judaism is not responsible for the events that occur in a life or in the world. Instead, Judaism acknowledges these events as part of the long journey of life. Using stories, virtues, practices, and rituals, Judaism supports and celebrates our individual, very personal wandering to the Promised Land.

I have come to believe that Judaism can hold all the beauty of our lives alongside the pain. Our individual, family, and communal stories, going all the way back to Adam and Eve, are all contained in an enormous vessel holding three thousand years of the Jewish story.

The vessel holding our stories is eternal, Rose. L'dor v'dor, from generation to generation, it's holding us together. And that, to me, makes Judaism positive.

Part Two

Jewish Well-Being in the Five Areas of Life

We now explore the pursuit of well-being in the five key areas of life—relationships, health, community, work, and money—and explore the role that Jewish virtues and practices play in this pursuit.

Think of Moses and the people of Israel as they wandered from slavery to freedom. They fled in the dark of night without time for their bread to rise, and they faced many hardships as they crisscrossed the desert in search of the land of milk and honey. We can imagine the strength it must have required to endure this journey.

This powerful memory is reenacted each year at Passover seder meals where participants imagine the toil of slavery and the forty-year march through the Sinai Desert. We eat the bread of affliction (matzah), taste the bitterness of oppression (*maror*), and dip into the tears of slavery (salt water). As this story is told and the foods are eaten, the participants become witness to the virtues that our ancestors displayed, such as resilience, bravery, and hope. Through this experience we can learn to embody these virtues in our lives. We draw on their power when faced with our own afflictions, bitterness, and tears. This has positive impact on character development and shows that the value of embracing ancient wisdom is not to live in the past, but to give context and meaning to the present.

Thus, it all begins with a story, the Jewish source for transmitting virtues and practices, and ultimately well-being and happiness.

In Part Two, we will explore a set of virtues and practices that are central to the Jewish experience. These same virtues and practices have been shown by science to be sources of happiness and well-being. In the chapters ahead we will:

- Explore the five areas of well-being—relationships, health, community, work, and money—from a Jewish perspective.
- Study five happiness virtues: resilience, optimism, loving-kindness, wisdom, and justice.
- Learn how these virtues are taught and deepened through the observance of Shabbat and the practices of prayer, community involvement, study, and giving charity.

At every step, we will consult research from the science of happiness and see how the three theories of well-being (PERMA, character strengths, and broaden-and-build) are activated within Jewish stories, holidays, and rituals.

3

"Love your neighbor as yourself."
—LEVITICUS 19:18

Relationships: Marriage, Family, and Parenting

Good relationships are essential to the flourishing life. People with high well-being have close relationships that help them achieve goals, enjoy life, and be healthy. They are surrounded by people who encourage their development and growth, accept them for who they are, and treat them with respect. They deliberately invest time in the networks of relationships that surround them.[40]

Ancient Jewish wisdom also places a high value on relationships, beginning with Adam and Eve. To encourage positive relationships, the Bible teaches, "Love your neighbor as yourself,"[41] and many of the Ten Commandments signal us to interact well with others. While many types of relationships have essential value to living well, we will explore three of the most common in this chapter: marriage and other committed relationships, family relationships, and parenting.

Take a moment and think about the people in your life who are the happiest. Studies would suggest that their happiness is directly connected to the quality of their relationships. This is not to say that generally unhappy people have no friendships or that having some bad relationships dooms one to unhappiness. Rather, two decades of research has revealed that people who spend time and energy to create and nurture positive relationships with partners, spouses, children, family, colleagues, neighbors, community, and themselves report high levels of well-being and life satisfaction.[42]

In Judaism, as elsewhere, relationships between significant others, spouses, extended family, and parents and children are at the center of living a meaningful life and hold an important role in happiness and well-being.

From Me to We: "Love Your Neighbor as Yourself"

To "love your neighbor as yourself" begins with understanding that you are at the center of your well-being and happiness. Everything you touch and everything you are or will be flows from the relationship you have with yourself. The Hebrew phrase is *bein adam l'atzmo*, "between a person and himself."

Martin Buber, a twentieth-century Jewish philosopher and author of the book *I and Thou*, taught that relationships hold the spiritual power to our happiness and well-being. His insight was that when we encounter another, we experience them from our perspective ("I") until we become aware that this other person ("Thou") is just like us, and we are like them. In other words, "Love your neighbor as yourself."

That awareness calls for a blend of real understanding, compassion, empathy, authenticity, and human connection, all occurring simultaneously. Thriving relationships have a "we" focus to them rather than a "me" focus. In positive psychology, this process is termed moving from "me to we."[43]

Buber's ideal of love has three elements. There is "I" and "Thou" and a third, hidden element within the I–Thou relationship that is represented by the dash (–). This is the divine element—the Absolute Revelation—which connects people together. In other words, when we are in authentic relationships with ourselves (I) and with another (Thou), the Divine is present (–). But when there is no real and honest bond (empty), there is no real and honest relationship.

Buber wrote, "In the pure relationship you felt altogether dependent, as you could never possibly feel in any other—and yet also altogether free as never and nowhere else; created—and creative. You no longer felt the one, limited by the other; you felt both without bonds, both at once."[44]

In the words of the Jewish French philosopher Emmanuel Levinas, "The face of my fellow man is an otherness which opens the door to the beyond."[45] Those who can learn to activate the I–Thou triad are on a path to high levels of well-being and happiness.

Positive Marriages and Committed Relationships

The Book of Proverbs teaches that an excellent partner is a jewel whose "worth is far beyond that of rubies."[46] The person we share our life with is our most important relationship. Research has revealed that people in long-term committed relationships are generally happier and healthier and have greater life satisfaction than single people.[47] In addition, they generally live, on average, ten years longer than single people or those in difficult relationships, which reinforces the biblical verse "It is not good for [people] to be alone."[48]

This does not mean that partners always feel happy and positive about their relationship. Similarly, it does not mean that single people cannot achieve the highest levels of happiness, joy, and well-being.

Jewish tradition teaches that when each of us is born, the Divine One assigns us a life partner. As we mature into adulthood, it is our fate to meet our match, our *bashert*. This takes patience, perhaps multiple relationships, even divorce, before we find our true love, our *bashert*. However, once connected, we discover the synergy of that relationship by recognizing that the purpose of our union is greater than either of us individually.

While *bashert* may be a traditional idea, we must be diligent in creating our own opportunities to find that special person. To believe that fate lives outside of our personal influence is to avoid taking full responsibility for our lives. While it is important to find the right person, it is more important to become the right person. Destiny is not passive; it is active.

Those passive about this very important relationship may be missing out on true happiness and well-being. Dr. John Gottman, an expert in marriage research, teaches, "True love is to revere each other and to be grateful that you are in each other's lives."[49] The *bashert* in our lives is our responsibility—as we are theirs—and so is discovering the higher purpose of the relationship.

The Higher Meaning of Jewish Weddings

Of all the beautiful rituals at a Jewish wedding, the last of the Sheva B'rachot (seven wedding blessings) and the breaking of the glass teach us most clearly about the purpose of marriage. The Sheva B'rachot conclude:

> Blessed are You, Eternal One, who illuminates the world with joy and happiness, love, a sublime joy, companionship, peace and friendship for the couple. May sounds of joy, song, happiness, and delight—the voices of this couple—be heard in Jewish communities and in Jerusalem. Blessed are You, Eternal One, who delights in the joy of this couple![50]

Since one purpose of married life is to experience happiness, joy, love, companionship, peace, and unity with a partner, what could be more instructive for a couple about the hopes and wishes that Judaism has for their future than the positive words of this marital blessing?

The breaking of the glass, the most recognizable Jewish wedding ritual, makes it even more significant. When the glass is broken at a Jewish wedding ceremony and the guests erupt in applause, it's about more than just celebrating the couple. Jewish mysticism endows a cosmic meaning to this seemingly simple act.

Rabbi Isaac Luria in the sixteenth century taught that at the beginning of time, God's presence filled the universe. When God decided to bring this world into being, and in order to make room for Creation, God first drew the divine breath into a single point. From that contraction, darkness was created. When God said, "Let there be light,"[51] the light that came into being filled the darkness, and ten holy vessels came forth, each filled with the light of Creation. However, these vessels were too fragile to contain such a powerful light, so they broke open and shattered, and all the holy sparks were scattered like the shards of light created by the broken glass.

The purpose of authentic love and commitment is to gather up these sparks—through acts of loving-kindness, for example—in order to create unity and wholeness in the relationship and subsequently in the universe. This is a *tikun*, a repair, and by fulfilling their unique purpose through their actions, the loving couple will contribute to repairing the universe, thereby raising the level of positivity in the world while simultaneously adding well-being and happiness to their own lives.

The Science of Happy Relationships

Happy relationships are not born, they are made. Creating a happy marriage and life partnership is more of an art than a science, yet there are specific elements of these relationships that have been studied in order to provide insight into what makes these couples thrive.

Think for a moment about the couples and marriages you admire. Marriages that are strong and supportive. Couples who are truly in love. Flourishing relationships. No doubt each relationship is different, and every couple is dealing with unique issues and pressures, but thriving couples have generally found a way to activate positivity, well-being, and happiness together.

In their own unique and dynamic way, strong and committed relationships have the elements of well-being at their core:

- They are consciously or unconsciously living expressions of **PERMA** (positive emotion, engagement, relationships, meaning, achievement).

- They know and value each other's **character strengths**.

- They find ways large and small to **broaden and build** the bond of their relationship.

Dr. John Gottman has created a scientific method to identify happy and unhappy couples. He focuses on marital conflict, because every couple manages their conflict differently, some more effectively than others.

Dr. Gottman's research shows that the difference between happy and unhappy couples can be seen in the balance between positive and negative interactions during conflict. The "magic ratio" is five to one. This means that for every negative interaction during conflict, a happy marriage has five (or more) positive interactions. Happy couples use skills—like humor, affection, and intentional listening—to cope with and resolve their problems.

On the other hand, unhappy couples engage in fewer positive interactions to resolve their issues. If the positive-to-negative ratio during conflict is one to one or less, that is a sign of an unhappy couple that could benefit greatly from learning positive skills to improve their bond.

Couples who have a positive ratio and manage their conflict well not only exhibit good relationship health, they also demonstrate that they know their purpose and have a shared vision for their destiny. Their intimacy is real, and they are improving the world through their love. In mystical terms, they are creating *tikun*, adding wholeness and unity, making their positive mark in the world.

Just as individuals are responsible for their own well-being, couples are responsible for their own happiness. Here are six proven activities for daily living that will increase a couple's well-being by naturally enhancing the healthy, supporting, and loving bond of their relationship.

1. **Talk more.** Happy couples spend at least five hours a week talking and being together without external interruptions. For starters, take the well-being surveys in the appendices of this book and discuss the results together.

2. **Express gratitude.** Happy couples regularly express their gratitude and appreciation for each other. Share words, cards, notes, and other small and large gifts of gratitude with each other. Many

choose to start their day, end their night, or begin their Shabbat dinners with a gratitude practice.

3. **Cultivate passion.** Passion in the bedroom gets cultivated outside the bedroom. Happy couples surprise each other, do novel activities, and share secrets with each other. Relive fun memories, give a compliment, and reaffirm your love. All of this will lead to greater intimacy.

4. **Mirror appreciation.** When your partner has an accomplishment or is recognized by others, acknowledge the achievement with genuine enthusiasm. Happy couples share the pride they have for each other's accomplishments among family, friends, and community.

5. **Seek joy.** Do novel and exciting activities together that boost happiness and joy and where you can relax and laugh together. Happy couples are good friends who enjoy sharing and creating fun times together.

6. **Forgive easily.** Happy couples choose not to sweat the small stuff and forgive easily. Let it go. Life is too short. Choose to forgive your spouse for something small and for something large. Tell your partner, "It's in the past," and move on.

The results of these activities will help a marriage or committed relationship flourish and will increase a couple's I–Thou bond. Most importantly, it will enhance the overall quality and level of well-being of their relationship.

The eighteenth-century Bershider Rabbi said, "Work for peace within your family, then in your street, then within the community." Thriving partnerships have peace in their home. The principle of *shalom bayit*, "peace in the home," is the Jewish ideal for having a strong and healthy relationship. The Talmud teaches that "anger in the home is like rottenness in fruit."[52] The opposite is also true: peace in the home is as sweet as apples and honey. As the Book of Psalms teaches, families should always try to "seek peace and pursue it."[53]

There are so many unique pressures on individuals, couples, and families today that maintaining a peaceful, committed, and loving relationship in the twenty-first century can feel like a Herculean effort, as we will see in the story of Richard and Jennifer.

"Rabbi, I Think I Married the Wrong Person": Meet Richard

Richard and his wife Jennifer are both in their mid-forties and have been married for sixteen years. They have three children. The years leading into their marriage were exceptionally happy. They were passionately in love, traveled with friends, and enjoyed sharing small and big moments together. They were aligned in their values and wanted to build a family.

However, things had changed. Richard was confused and wondered silently whether he had made the right decision to marry Jennifer. Their lightweight spats were growing more intense. When Jennifer got pregnant, he was excited to be a father but was growing unsure about the quality of their marriage. After the baby was born, their entire relationship became child-centric. Lately, he had been drinking more, making mistakes at work, and been tempted to start an affair with one of his clients.

"Rabbi, I think I married the wrong person. I don't get Jennifer anymore. What's happened to her? She's angry and stressed all the time. Now it's always the kids. It's like her whole life is 'the kids.' I feel totally alone in this marriage."

Like every family-minded person, Richard wants to be happy in his marriage, but he's confused about how to find that happiness. I shared a story with him.

The Maggid of Dubnov would often speak of a king who had the most beautiful diamond. Every night, the king would look at this diamond and marvel at its perfection. One night, to his horror, he dropped the diamond onto the floor, and a small crack appeared from the base of the diamond all the way to the crown.

Brokenhearted, he summoned the best craftsmen to repair his diamond. One after the other told him, no, once a diamond is cracked, it is not repairable. The king called for anyone who could repair his jewel to report to the castle. Days later, a humble jeweler came forward and volunteered to repair the diamond. "How can you fix this when all others have failed?" asked the king. The jeweler assured him that he could, but the king warned him, "If you fix this, I will give you great riches, but if you fail, you will be killed for deceiving me."

The man went to his workshop and set himself to the task. Days later, the jeweler returned to the king with the diamond. With trembling hands, the king took the diamond, unwrapped it, and to his fury, the crack was still there. "Take this man to the gallows!" screamed the king. But the man stood calmly and asked the king to turn the diamond over.

Turning it over, the king saw that at the top of the diamond, the man had carved two petals, so now the crack was not a flaw but the stem of a flower, making his "broken" diamond even more perfect, beautiful, and unique.

I hoped Richard and Jennifer could imagine a life that put their love for each other at the center of their family, despite all the pressures and stresses in their daily lives. Positive relationships take work, but with a little help, a cracked diamond can become a flower, more beautiful than before.

Studies have shown that parents with young children at home face incredible pressures. Despite the joys of parenthood, many say that it is the most unhappy time of their lives, with the greatest strain on their marriage and their physical health.[54] Evidence shows that people forty to fifty years old with kids find this the most difficult decade of their lives, with the competing pressures of family and work.[55] It can feel unbearable at times.

It's natural for people to seek relief from these pressures. Some folks sabotage their marriages by having affairs. Others turn to drugs and alcohol to numb the pressure. These pathways only add to the problems at home and create new problems at work. Even if one partner may feel like Richard and think they married the wrong person, there is lasting value in finding ways to keep a relationship alive and to keep a family intact. In addition to the proven tools listed earlier, activating character strengths can also improve the relationship. Among the many strengths available, resilience is an important one to elevate when we feel the stresses of life mounting against us.

The Gift of Resilience

Life is full of raindrops, some larger than others, but everyone gets wet. Yet, the science of well-being shows time and again that resilient people can better withstand life's inevitable storms, even emerge from them wiser and stronger.[56]

Resilience is a character strength that is learned from the people in our lives and the relationships we have with them. The Hebrew word for resilience is *ko'ach*. It is common to say to someone following their reading from Torah or giving an excellent Torah lesson, *Yasher ko'ach*, "May you have resilience/strength."

Resilience is the ability to remain active, energetic, focused, and flexible no matter the situation. Studies show that resilient people are emotionally agile. They neither steel themselves against negativity nor wallow in it.[57]

JEWISH HAPPINESS VIRTUE
RESILIENCE
Resilience, *ko'ach*, is the ability to remain active, energetic, focused, and flexible no matter the situation.

Judaism is a great teacher of resilience because at the heart of Jewish traditions, rituals, and holidays is the story of how relationships among a people, the Jewish people, *Am Yisrael*, were preserved and strengthened by the ability to bounce back from adversity.

Thriving Families

Just as couples have a destiny and a higher purpose to their relationship, so do families. While the higher purpose of a Jewish couple is to create love, the higher purpose of the family is to build on this foundation of love and to create peace in the home. Yet, in a world where families face so many complex issues, how can they find a way to elevate the family experience?

The late Rabbi Menachem Schneerson, leader of Lubavitch Chasidism held that "the home should be perceived as a microcosm of the universe: The harmony that permeates the home and the family extends beyond, fostering harmony between families, communities and ultimately, the nations of the world. In the absence of harmony between one's own family, we can hardly expect to find harmony between strangers."

Seeking harmony is a marvelous ideal, yet I find that few families have a framework for how to achieve it. I would like to suggest our first theory of well-being—PERMA—as a pathway to *shalom bayit*, peace in the home.

The first element of PERMA is **positive emotion**. In a family environment that is full of positive emotion, its members feel loved, supported, and safe. This does not mean that every interaction needs to be positive and joyful. There are arguments and disagreements in all families, but similar to the ratio that measures the health of a couple, the goal within families should also be a 5:1 ratio, five positive interactions to every negative one. This is one sign of a healthy and thriving family.

Finding ways for the family to **engage** together adds well-being to their family life. Eating meals, playing games, building projects, exploring parks, attending school events, and going to synagogue are some ways that families develop shared interests and positively engage with one another.

Among family **relationships**, it is the parents who model the qualities they want their children to adopt. Parents who freely express their love in calm and supportive ways will create an environment where children feel safe, loved, and supported, thus broadening and building healthy family relationships.

Positive **meaning** within the family unit rests upon a values environment established actively or passively by the parents. How a family embraces education, community, religion, materialism, and so on impacts the type of meaning that is created within the family unit.

The last element of PERMA that can raise a family's well-being is based on the shared goals they actively seek to **accomplish** together. This can begin with creating a chores wheel where each family member takes responsibility for doing a household task. It might grow into a family aspiring to prepare meals together on certain nights, volunteering at the local homeless shelter on holidays, or discovering their own shared vision of their greater purpose.

Positive Jewish Parenting

When my children were younger, I spent a lot of time with them at playgrounds and in parks. While watching them play, negotiate, and get dirty, I learned a lot about parenting styles by observing other parents attend to their children. One mother stood out to me, with her constant praise for her daughter. "Becca, your rock pile is amazing!" "Wow, your slide down was amazing!" "Darling, your hold on the monkey bars was amazing!" Her enthusiasm was admirable, and praise parenting does have value, but a different approach to positive parenting, called strengths-based parenting, may have even better, more long-term results.

Every parent wants their child to be happy, healthy, and successful in their lives. We want each child to be a mensch, a good person, and to have a positive impact in the world. Yet, some children evolve into thriving adults while others live unfulfilled lives. Many factors obviously lead to this difference, but one of the most essential tools a parent can give their child is the ability to identify and develop their signature strengths over the course of their lives.

Want a Mensch? Develop Your Child's Signature Strengths

Two thousand years ago, the Jewish sages instructed that "every parent must teach their child to swim."[58] Some sages interpret this to mean that a parent must teach a child to survive and be responsible for themselves. The best pathway to teaching a child to swim and creating a mensch is to develop their positive character strengths.

Parenting expert Dr. Lea Waters defines strengths as "positive qualities that energize us and that we use often in productive ways to achieve our goals. They are developed over time and are recognized by others as praiseworthy."[59] Strengths-based parenting focuses on children's character strengths (e.g., optimism, creativity, gratitude, resilience),[60] rather than their accomplishments or their incremental weaknesses. It's about learning how to help our children use their strengths to complete an activity and to sustain their attention. Strengths-based parenting works like this:

- "Honey, I can see how much **creativity** you brought to this art project," rather than "This art project is wonderful!"

- "Wow! That took a lot of **restraint** and **courage**. I can imagine it was hard not to throw that insult back at him," rather than "I know he was being a jerk. Kids are jerks sometimes."

- "Jennifer, you **accomplished** so much by getting a 94 on your math exam—well done," rather than "What happened with that one you got wrong? You could have gotten a perfect score if you used what we practiced last night."

Instead of focusing on weaknesses and external factors, strengths-based parenting focuses on positive character development. A research scientist may view this approach to parenting as putting your kids in touch with their unique constellation of talents and character. A rabbi may view strengths-based parenting as teaching a child to swim. The scientist and the rabbi are both saying the same thing: parents who actively identify and develop their child's strengths will help them thrive with the following proven results:[61]

- Greater levels of happiness and engagement at school

- Higher levels of academic achievement

- Higher levels of physical fitness and healthy lifestyles

- Increased levels of life satisfaction and self-esteem

- Reduced risk of depression and enhanced ability to cope with stress and diversity

Parenting my own children is the most important part of my life. As they've grown, it's become clear to me that to be effective, I need to grow as a parent at a similar pace. The biggest challenges came when my eldest son, Emmett, became a teenager. The little boy was still in there, but the speed of his emotional, intellectual, and physical changes made it seem like he had become a young man overnight. This young man wanted more privacy and more freedom, which I was delighted to see, but I knew it would require some new strategies for each of us.

He was eager to have more independence. I was eager for him to have new insights and tools in order to thrive and be a mensch. A fifteen-minute online survey called the VIA Youth Survey (www.viacharacter.org) helped us discover and learn about his signature strengths. This has given him new approaches to solve problems and to make more effective decisions. To paraphrase the Book of Proverbs, "My [child], if you accept my words and treasure up my commandments; if you make your ear attentive to wisdom and your mind open to discernment; if you call to understanding and cry aloud to discernment, if you seek it as you do silver and search for it as for treasures, then you will understand [your signature strengths and how to use them for your best life possible]."[62]

Experience Shabbat

Israeli poet Achad Ha'am said, "As much as the Jewish people have kept the Shabbat, Shabbat has kept the Jewish people."

Shabbat lasts from sundown on Friday to sundown on Saturday, and there are many ways to separate this day from the rest of the week and to make it special. How can we use the invitation of Shabbat to raise the quality of our happiness and well-being?

Shabbat offers a weekly opportunity to strengthen relationships, transmit family values, and deepen *shalom bayit*, peace in the home. Shabbat traditions include sharing festive meals, worshipping with community at synagogue, spending quiet time with family at home, and visiting with family and friends. These weekly traditions encourage togetherness and quality time, and so help build and strengthen relationships.

There are many unique and creative ways to observe Shabbat. We can prepare and eat meals together, take walks in nature, spend time on family hobbies and interests. Finding time to nourish yourself and recharge your strengths will add value to the important relationships in your life, especially the relationship you have with yourself and the people closest to you.

For Personal Reflection

1. In what ways can you apply the lesson of the flawed diamond to the difficult relationships in your own life?

2. How can a Shabbat experience serve as a pathway to boost the well-being of the most important relationships in your life?

3. How could activating character strengths like resilience raise the harmony in your home and in the life of your family?

4

"Be extremely protective of your lives."
—DEUTERONOMY 4:15

Health: Physical and Mental Well-Being

I grew up in a home where if you had an emotion, you would eat. And we ate. A lot. I think the reaction my parents had to my physical size growing up was "Healthy—he's got a healthy appetite." But that all changed on the day my father took me shopping for my bar mitzvah suit.

It happened over thirty years ago, but I remember it like yesterday. It was a rite of passage for him, taking me to the suit warehouse in Downtown Los Angeles, where he and "every" boy got their special suit. Surrounded by rows upon rows of suits, the old man of the factory took one look at me and said, "No regular suits for him. Too big in the *tuchas* [Yiddish for rear end]."

With a little creativity, the old man and my father eventually paired a blazer and slacks for my bar mitzvah uniform, but that episode changed us. Unlike today, back then the general public knew much less about health and the impact that sugar, preservatives, carbohydrates, packaged foods, and soda had on our bodies. Though still a work in progress, 1985 was the year I started to change the way I approached food, to what would be considered today a cleaner diet.

"Maintaining a healthy and sound body is among the ways of the Divine," taught Moses Maimonides about one thousand years ago, "for one cannot understand or have any knowledge of the Creator if one is ill. Therefore, one must avoid that which harms the body and accustom oneself to that which is helpful and helps the body become stronger."[63] Ancient wisdom is clear: put effort into building a healthy and strong body.

Modern science makes the same claim. "People with thriving physical wellbeing manage their health well. They exercise regularly and feel better throughout the day as a result. They make good dietary choices, which keeps their energy high throughout the day and sharpens their thinking. They get enough sleep to wake up feeling well-rested and to process what they have learned the day before—and to get a good start on the next day."[64]

When it comes to the impact of physical health on a person's well-being, ancient wisdom and modern science are in agreement. But what about mental health? What is the impact that our thoughts and feelings have on our overall health, and therefore our level of happiness and well-being?

Elements of Positive Health

Today, advancements in mind-body awareness and better education have put the importance of good health and psychological well-being at center stage. We know that diet, exercise, sleep, and stress have a huge impact on our physical and emotional well-being. We know that sugar, artificial ingredients, hormone-boosted foods, smoking, and excessive alcohol can damage our bodies. For some these have become addictions, but with the treatments available today, everyone has the ability to invest more time and energy in raising the quality of their physical health.

The nineteenth-century intellectual leader Rabbi Samson Raphael Hirsch wrote that a person "may not in any way weaken his health or shorten his life. Only if the body is healthy can it be an instrument for the spirit's activity [of prayer]. . . . Therefore one should avoid everything which might possibly injure their health."[65]

The great twelfth-century philosopher Moses Maimonides takes it one step further. For him, good health is more than just avoiding that which harms the body, but rather is the result of actively building strength. "A person should accustom oneself to that which is helpful and helps the body become stronger."[66] Here are three Jewish teachings that inspire positive physical health:

1. **Food and nutrition:** The Torah teaches that each person was "created in the divine image."[67] If we believe that our bodies are a sacred gift, we should be inspired to fuel them with clean foods that nourish, rather than heavily processed and manufactured foods that may be full of chemicals.

2. **Exercise and fitness:** The wise sage Chofetz Chayim taught that "the entire Torah is dependent on the mitzvah of taking care of your body."[68] Maimonides said that caring for the body comes first, "so as long as one exercises and exerts himself vigorously . . . no illness will befall him and his physical powers will be strengthened."[69]

3. **Live clean:** In the first century, the beloved teacher Hillel once told his students that he was off to complete a good deed. When they asked, "Where are you going?" he replied, "I'm going to bathe. If even the stone statues of kings are washed and scrubbed clean, how much more so should we humans keep our bodies clean."[70] This teaches us not only to be smart with what we choose to put inside our bodies, but how we treat the exterior of our body as well.

Jewish tradition teaches that much of our physical well-being is within our own influence. Positive health may be felt in the body, but it starts in the mind and can be influenced by being optimistic about our health and our future. Just as we can choose to have a strong body through diet, exercise, and living clean, optimism is also a choice. The good news is that not only can optimism be learned, but that living a Jewish life promotes an optimistic mind-set, which has a direct influence on our physical health.

The Power of Optimism on Health

People who have a strong sense of optimism and a positive mind-set are demonstrably happier, physically healthier, and cope better with life stress than those with more pessimistic views.[71] It's been shown that optimism has a positive effect on the immune system and that optimists have fewer illnesses and diseases.[72] Studies have found that optimistic thinking promotes positive moods, vitality, and high morale.[73] Optimists do better in sports, perform better in the classroom, and go farther in their careers, while pessimism and negative mind-sets keep people stuck in unhappiness.[74]

The Hebrew word for "optimism" is *tikvah*, which also means "hope." "Hatikvah," "The Hope," is the national anthem of Israel and the Jewish people. Hope and optimism are also central themes in the Book of Psalms: "As for me, I will hope always, and add to the many praises of You."[75]

> **JEWISH HAPPINESS VIRTUE: OPTIMISM**
>
> Optimism, *tikvah*, is a mind-set that believes goodness will come forth from any given situation.

Optimism is a mind-set that believes goodness will come forth from any given situation. An important virtue for maintaining a positive attitude, optimism contrasts with helplessness, the belief that we have no control over what occurs in life. Dr. Martin Seligman, the expert in learned optimism, teaches that the skills of optimism do not emerge from happy events or from learning to say positive things to yourself. Rather, what is crucial is what you think when you fail and how you use the power of non-negative thinking. Changing the destructive messages you say to yourself when you experience setbacks in life is the central skill of optimism.[76]

Optimism Can Be Learned

One of the claims of Positive Judaism is that our strengths and abilities are both inherited from our genetic code and learned and developed by life experience. Optimism is a good example. Optimism may be something we inherit, but it's also a virtue that we can learn in the journey to greater wellness.[77] To grow in optimism, there are specific ways to understand and explain the events in our lives. For instance, pessimistic people often view the negative events of their lives as their own personal fault and the result of their own weakness. On the other hand, optimistic people relate the negative events in their lives to the specific experience only, rather than seeing them as overall statements of their character.

For example, my youngest son, Adrian, loves acting and singing, and he regularly auditions for shows at our neighborhood community theater. Sometimes he gets a role, but more often he does not get the part he wants. Over the years, we have helped him learn to be optimistic about the audition process. He is disappointed when he does not get chosen for a role, but he's learned to explain it to himself with an optimistic mind-set.

I remember overhearing a fellow young actor in his group talking to her mother after a recent cast announcement. She said, "I knew I wasn't going to get that part. I'm terrible at auditions. I'll never get good parts." This is a pessimistic explanatory style about the bad things that happen in life. The girl took it personally and made broad negative claims about her acting ability.

My son Adrian, on the other hand, reacted differently. He read the same cast list and did not see his name either. But rather than default into pessimism, he said, "There were a lot of good actors at the audition. That audition was unique because they had us do a lot of dancing, and I did not expect that. I'll just have to prepare differently next time." He displayed an optimistic explanatory style. Adrian interpreted this event not as a global statement about his acting ability, but rather as a singular experience.

Where does Adrian get his optimism? He inherited part of it from our family, and the other part comes from how he has learned to frame and to explain the experiences in his life. I believe much of his learned optimism, and my own, comes from our knowledge of Jewish wisdom and the stories we tell from our tradition.

An Optimistic Mind-Set Can Change the World

Nobody is immune to the real challenges of life. Optimists and pessimists face these same challenges every day—problems at work, difficulties with children and parents, or their own personal worries, for example. The difference is that the optimist views life's difficulties with the hope of better things to come, while the pessimist, who may not have the tools and confidence to bounce back, sees only trouble and more of it on the horizon.

The good news is that pessimists can change. Pessimists can learn the skills and develop the strengths that optimists have in order to improve their lives. As the late prime minister of Israel Golda Meir said, "Pessimism is a luxury that a Jew can never allow himself."[78]

The following is a story of how a well-known, skeptical pessimist changed his mind-set and thereby changed the course of history.

The setting was a summit meeting at Camp David, September 1978. The players: United States president Jimmy Carter, Israeli prime minister Menachem Begin, and Egyptian president Anwar Sadat.[79]

The purpose of this summit was to create a peace deal between Egypt and Israel, but the cards were stacked against each of these men. Jimmy Carter was at one of the lowest points in his national approval ratings, highly unpopular among the American people. Anwar Sadat was a Nazi sympathizer and an admitted terrorist. Menachem Begin was a Holocaust survivor, known by everyone to be obstinate and pessimistic. In the past thirty years, Begin and Sadat had lived through four wars between their countries.

This summit was a thirteen-day rollercoaster of diplomacy. As the men and their governments drew close to an agreement, Begin backpedaled on a previously agreed upon point, followed by Sadat, who did the same. Menachem Begin told President Carter that it was over and went back to his cabin to pack. At the table of history, Begin was about to walk away.

President Carter was incensed.

Begin was unaware that the day before, Carter's secretary had called an Israeli friend for the names of Begin's nine grandchildren. President Carter had signed a photo of himself with Sadat and Begin at Camp David, personalizing it for each of the grandchildren. President Carter had an optimistic mind-set that imagined a future for peace.

As Begin was packing up, President Carter stopped in to say goodbye. In his southern way, Carter thanked Begin for coming, shook hands, handed him an envelope, and said, "Menachem, this is for your grandchildren." Begin opened the thick envelope containing the signed copies of the historic photo. Carter said, "I was hoping they would remember you as being the man who brought peace to Israel."

Carter hugged him goodbye and returned to his Camp David office. Ten minutes later his phone rang. It was Begin. He said two words, "I'll sign."

That was a watershed moment for the history of the Middle East and for Begin. Forty years later, that peace accord still holds, and Begin's grandchildren remember him as the man who made peace with Egypt. An unlikely story, but true, and one that took courage, hope, and most importantly, optimism.

Jewish Wisdom Teaches Optimism

The Chasidic master Tzemech Tzedak said, "Think good and it will be good." But how do we learn to "think good"? One way is by developing an optimistic mind-set and deepening self-awareness.

In the study of Judaism, we learn that optimism is the foundation of many stories and that many biblical characters have an optimistic explanatory style. One example is the story of Moses and the scouts. Prior to entering the Land of Israel, Moses sent twelve scouts to survey the new land and report back to him. When the group returned, ten of the scouts said, "The country that we traversed and scouted is one that devours its settlers. All the people that we saw in it are men of great size; like giants . . . and we looked like grasshoppers to ourselves, and so we must have looked to them."[80] These scouts were pessimistic, seeing only the dangers in the land.

Then Moses turned to Joshua and Caleb, who reported, "The land that we traversed and scouted is an exceedingly good land . . . a land that flows with milk and honey. . . . Have no fear!"[81] They believed they would thrive in the Land of Israel. Their attention was focused on the goodness and future bounty of the land. Joshua and Caleb displayed an optimistic explanatory style, and Moses granted them the highest reward: to enter the Land of Israel after forty years in the wilderness, and to succeed him as the leaders of a new generation.

That was an important turning point in the story of the Israelites on their journey to the Promised Land, and an important message from the Torah about optimism. Could you imagine the result if Moses allowed himself to be influenced and directed by the ten voices of pessimism? Like Prime Minister Begin at Camp David, the outcome of history would have been very different.

Jewish Prayer Develops Optimism

In addition to studying the Bible and learning history, another way to increase optimism and self-awareness is through prayer and developing our spiritual lives. A groundbreaking study on the health benefits of prayer found that being spiritual and having faith are elements that lead people to feel happier, be physically healthier, and cope better with life stress.[82] One researcher concluded that "the emotional power of ritual is transmitted in sacred community and feelings of higher connection are formed and deepened in sacred moments and spaces, and this has a positive effect in the lives of individuals and communities."[83]

T'filah is the Hebrew word for "prayer," and prayer has been shown to teach, instill, and inspire optimism and gratitude.[84] In fact, much of Jewish prayer is focused upon peace and hope for the future. In the Wisdom of Solomon we find, "Wherefore I prayed, and understanding was given me: I called upon God, and the spirit of wisdom came to me."[85]

> There is a tale about a boy who came to a synagogue for the very first time on Yom Kippur, the holiest day of the year. He walked into the sanctuary and heard all the prayers and the people reciting them in unison. He sat in the back of the room, put on a skullcap, and opened a prayer book. To his dismay, he could not read a

single word of Hebrew, but he did recognize the letters *alef* and *bet* as he skimmed the text. Wanting to feel connected to the group and not be seen as an outsider, he started to repeat the letters, "*Alef bet alef bet alef bet.*"

One of the synagogue's regular members tapped the rabbi's shoulder during a break. "Rabbi, there is a boy at the back who is just saying, '*Alef bet alet bet alef bet.*' He's not praying like us." The rabbi turned to the back of the room, smiled warmly at the boy, then whispered to the man, "Every sound uttered with true conviction is prayer. God knows how to turn the sounds into honest prayer."

JEWISH WELL-BEING PRACTICE
Prayer and Personal Reflection

In Jewish practice, there are two approaches to prayer: fixed prayer (*keva*) and personal prayer (*kavanah*). Fixed prayers are the ones in a prayer book that follow a rigid outline. Personal prayer is open-hearted prayer that may focus on a theme like gratitude, hope, or thanksgiving. It might also be a heartfelt prayer for your own desires or wishes or for the health and well-being of another person, like a child, family member, or dear friend. These personal prayers are like meditations of the heart and play an important role in developing a person's sense of optimism and other character strengths that encourage well-being.

Jewish prayers that acknowledge the profound and holistic nature of our human bodies bring us closer to the spiritual essence of our physical well-being. Asher Yatzar, one of the daily morning prayers, gives thanks for vitality:

> Blessed are You, Eternal One of the universe, who fashioned humans with wisdom, and created within each human many openings and many cavities. It is obvious and known before Your throne of glory that if but one

of them were to be ruptured, or but one of them were to be blocked, it would be impossible to survive and to stand before You. Blessed are You, Eternal One, who heals all flesh and acts wondrously.

Praying with others or feeling inspired to pray individually is a very personal matter. Whether you believe in God or not, setting aside regular time to express gratitude for your body's systems, your health, and all that is right with the world is a proven way to build well-being. Jewish tradition teaches that a person should say one hundred prayers a day, acknowledging the importance of expressing appreciation and gratitude.

In addition to attending formal prayer gatherings, there are a number of Jewish ways to practice personal prayer on your own. A few examples include saying aloud a word of appreciation for life and health upon waking in the morning, expressing gratitude for nourishment at the beginning of a meal, and acknowledging the gift of life when you see or experience something that you recognize as profound.

For Personal Reflection

1. In what ways could you imagine that optimism could increase your physical and emotional well-being?

2. What is one area of your life that could benefit by bringing more optimism to it?

3. How could prayer create an optimistic and hopeful sense of the future for you?

5

"Do not separate yourself from the community."

—HILLEL (FIRST-CENTURY SAGE), PIRKEI AVOT 2:4

Community: Bringing People Together

To be Jewish is to be with people and to be connected to community. After all, ancient wisdom teaches that the people of Israel were birthed in community during the generation that wandered in the Sinai Desert.

Similarly, modern research shows that "people with high well-being take pride in their community and feel that it is headed in the right direction. This often results in their wanting to give back and make a lasting contribution to society."[86]

Both ancient wisdom and modern science place a high value on the connections people have with their community and their state of happiness and well-being. Yet, despite this, we live in a world where loneliness and feelings of isolation, particularly within the younger generations, are at record levels.[87] What can be done to address this concern and to help people bind themselves to community and grow in well-being? We must create communities that place individual and communal well-being as the top priority and then engage people in deep ways to help them grow in positive and meaningful directions.

The Value of Positive Community: Meet Sylvia

Seymour regularly attended my lunchtime Torah study class for retirees. A sweet man, well into his mid-eighties, he arrived early, took the same seat, and ate the same lunch. Then, like clockwork, he'd close his eyes and take a nap. As the session concluded, he'd wake up, thank me, and head out to meet his wife, Sylvia, who was waiting to pick him up.

But one day, Sylvia called to tell me that Seymour had suffered a fatal heart attack. He had wanted me to officiate his funeral, and she had questions.

It's very disorienting when family members die, but Judaism has a set of communal practices that are designed to help people stay connected to life even when they are surrounded by death. At a Jewish funeral, specific prayers and psalms are recited, eulogies are shared, and the deceased is lowered into a grave. It's customary for those present, young and old, to take turns shoveling earth onto the lowered casket. Everyone who steps to the edge of a gravesite and shovels earth learns the lessons of life and death. There's no avoiding the moment of seeing your own destiny when you look six feet down.

Once the grave has been filled, the Mourner's Kaddish, a prayer that affirms life, is recited: *Yitgadal v'yitkadash, sh'mei rabbah*, "May God's great name be exalted and sanctified." Then the community stands face to face in two long lines. A human pathway is created from the grave outward through which the family members exit the cemetery.

Now begins the time of shiva (the weeklong mourning period). In many synagogue communities, members coordinate meals, child care, even financial support, to help the mourners manage all the practical aspects of life so that they can focus on their most important task: mourning their loss. Death happens to an individual, bereavement falls to the survivors, but the entire community steps up to support and comfort.

This is what Sylvia experienced when her beloved Seymour died.

Three weeks after the funeral, she told me, "Rabbi, I never quite appreciated the value of community until my Seymour died. My parents had a difficult life. I'm not a believer and never sought out a place in Judaism. But that's changed now.

"People from the synagogue came to visit me. They brought food. They insisted on running errands for me. I'm a rather private person, but I liked the attention. It took my mind off constantly thinking of Seymour."

Synagogue bereavement groups are some of the most valued structures in the Jewish community. The attentiveness that community can bring to a bereaved spouse, like Sylvia, serves as a positive influence to help survivors stay focused on living and the future.

Over time, Sylvia became more involved in the synagogue and made friends with other widows. One afternoon she showed up to my lunch-and-learn Torah study group. She was always very attentive, didn't say much, and if I remember correctly, never once fell asleep.

Engagement with Community Brings Well-Being and Happiness

A significant cultural study comparing levels of happiness among people who participated in religious community versus those who did not found a direct link between one's involvement in community and a person's well-being.[88] When I was a child, I always felt good surrounded by my Jewish community, whether at temple, social gatherings, summer camp, youth group, or while visiting Jewish groups abroad. The same is true today. I feel more alive, more connected to others, and more known and understood when I am actively participating in Jewish communal activities.

This is how many people feel about their community. Even culturally based movements like Burning Man and Grateful Dead concerts help people feel connected. Among their own community, people experience a closeness and resonate at a higher emotional frequency. In fact, happiness has been shown to be contagious within communities, and positivity can spread like a virus.[89]

However, there is a unique element that has been found among participants of religious communities. The research shows that people who participate in religious communities are happier and physically healthier than people with no religious participation in six specific ways. Researchers found that religion:[90]

- Provides social support.

- Supports healthy lifestyles.

- Promotes personality integration.

- Promotes altruism and humility.

- Provides important coping strategies.

- Provides a sense of meaning and purpose.[91]

We know that people feel happier and more positive about their lives when activating their signature strengths, and successful religious communities create space for people to express those strengths in a safe and loving environment. It's been shown that people can best express their most human values (e.g., optimism, kindness, gratitude) and appreciate and develop their psychological strengths (e.g., resilience, humility, forgiveness) while part of a religious community.[92]

In the most positive case, participating in sacred community teaches people to love humanity, find support in times of need, and provide love that heals. Religious community is a place that has a sanctuary and where people can find sanctuary. It's the place for friendship, for acceptance, for learning, and for discovering a meaningful life. Community is the antidote to loneliness and social isolation, and while these truths are valid in many religious communities, there are some unique qualities about Judaism that lead specifically to well-being and happiness.

The Jewish People Were Birthed in Community

The people of Israel began as a community of slaves in Egypt, many generations after our Jewish story began with our ancestors Abraham and Sarah. The Torah recounts that hundreds of thousands of Israelite slaves were rescued by Moses with God's help. They were a tribe, a collective, a community. To this day, every Jew is directly connected to that ancient tribe, that community of slaves. Thus began the story of the Jewish people, a three-thousand-year-old community.

The Jewish people are more than a religious group. We are a nation, a community with roots all over the world. There are Jews in the West and the East. There are Jews in Africa and Asia. There are Jews on Copacabana Beach and in the northern regions of Alaska. Among the Jewish people today, there are dozens of native languages, cultures, and ways of identifying Jewishly. All Jews are connected, and in the words of the Talmud, "All Jews are responsible for one another."[93]

Some of my most special memories of the Jewish community have been created during my travels. In my early twenties, I did a lot of low budget traveling and would often find myself in a different city on a Friday. One of the first things I would do in the morning is ask around for a Jewish synagogue or group that met for Shabbat that night.

I may have been a tourist, but once I arrived at the local synagogue, I felt at home. I was no longer a visitor; I was with my community to share an ancient tradition. With members of the congregation and, at times, fellow travelers, we'd play the well-known game Jewish Geography.

It was fun as we struggled to communicate with each other in our native tongues, but that was beside the point. I was their brother from the United States, and I was family. Whenever I travel, I still make a point to visit Jewish heritage sites. At the same time, it's a great honor to welcome visitors and guests to my congregation in New York City, where we teach that welcome is a spiritual practice.

Loving-Kindness Is the Greater Purpose of the Jewish Community

Simeon the Righteous (second century) was one of the last of the men of the Great Assembly. He would say, "The world is based upon three things: Torah, divine service, and acts of loving-kindness [g'milut chasadim]."[94]

Loving-kindness is a character strength that describes our ability to be compassionate, nurturing, caring, generous with others, and able to do good deeds altruistically. Without loving-kindness, we become indifferent and self-centered.

The Psalmist calls our attention to the vision that "goodness and kindness shall follow me all the days of my life."[95] God is described in the prayer book as having boundless loving-kindness: "Great is the virtue of love and kindness because it is one of the thirteen attributes ascribed to God. As it is written: 'God, compassionate and gracious, slow to anger, abounding in love and kindness.'"[96] So, the notion that communities can be places that embody loving-kindness is deeply rooted in Torah and tradition.

The synagogue, the day school, and the Jewish Community Center remain the active places for Jewish life today. Enhancing these primary structures to promote the growth of community are institutions like Jewish summer camps, Hillel on college campuses, federations like United Jewish Appeal, and unions of the Reform, Conservative, Reconstructionist, and Orthodox movements, and seminaries.

Beyond these structures, organizations like Jewish Family Services, Bureaus of Jewish Education, homes for the aged, and *bikur cholim* and *chevrah kaddisha* societies that visit the ill and lovingly support the deceased are highly valued resources. Philanthropic foundations, Israel advocacy associations, and groups that support social, racial, and economic justice play an important role. Added to these institutions are new programs like Birthright Israel, Maccabi USA Sports for Israel, PJ Library, Hazon, Repair the World, and Jewish farms. All of these are important organizations to support Jewish community in the twenty-first century.

I am very hopeful and optimistic for Judaism in the twenty-first century and believe the best is yet to come. Judaism and Jewish community offer a timeless wisdom and a powerful sense of connection in an era when people are feeling more isolated by the impersonality of machines and the seeming disarray of our political world. People are looking for real connections, authentic friendships, and genuine community. I think that, with some positive changes, the Jewish community is primed to be the place that offers people all this and more.

Faith Community: The Place for Well-Being and Happiness

In chapter 3, we discussed that the home is an ideal place to create and develop PERMA (positive emotions, engagement, relationships, meaning, accomplishment) in the life of a family. Similarly, the community is where these qualities of well-being are further cultivated and nourished among individuals and families in a collective. And while *shalom bayit*, peace in the home, is the greater purpose of the family, teaching and experiencing loving-kindness is the greater purpose of a faith community. Loving-kindness, *g'milut chasadim*, is the ability to be compassionate, nurturing, caring, generous with others, and able to do good deeds altruistically.

Jewish organizations that put well-being and loving-kindness at their center will be doing a great service for the individuals and families in their communities. People who never felt welcomed by the Jewish community will be embraced by the open heart of loving-kindness. At the same time, active participants will learn to embody the character of loving-kindness in their lives, which will influence their ability to be open-minded, flexible, and accepting of differences.

> **JEWISH HAPPINESS VIRTUE**
> **LOVING-KINDNESS**
> Loving-kindness, *g'milut chasadim*, is the ability to be compassionate, nurturing, caring, generous with others, and able to do good deeds altruistically.

Loving-kindness can mean different things to different people in different settings at different times, but it was captured best by Rabbi Menachem Mendel Schneerson, the Lubavitcher Rebbe, who said, "To be kind is more important than to be right. Many times, what people need is not a brilliant mind that speaks, but a heart that listens." A community filled with the spirit of open hearts that listens to its people is the most important thing that can be offered in the twenty-first century.

How do we instill the strength of loving-kindness in our communities for all to benefit? Six Jewish sages were asked this very question over two thousand years ago, and to this day their answers hold a great deal of truth:

> The sage Rabbi Yochanan said to his students, "Go out and see which is the good way that a person should live." Rabbi Eliezer said, "A good eye." Rabbi Yehoshua said, "A good friend." Rabbi Yossi said, "A good neighbor." Rabbi Shimon said, "One who foresees the result of an action." And lastly, Rabbi Elazar said, "A good heart." [Yochanan] said to them: "I prefer the words of Elazar . . . for in his words yours are included."[97]

Prudence (a good eye), close personal relationships (a good friend), civility (a good neighbor), acumen (foresee the result of an action), and loving-kindness (a good heart) are the essential qualities that lead to a happy life.

Communities that put loving-kindness at the center have deep obligations to their people and to humanity. They create and build an ethos of happiness and well-being in the ways they organize and make decisions. Staff and boards are trained to accomplish this within their community, and they commit to improving the collective and individual lives of their members.

Similarly, members of a congregation as a whole also have obligations to the health of their community. It must work in both directions. Jewish communities should strive to become centers of happiness, positivity, and well-being; and once individuals know that their community is committed to these ideals, people will show up in numbers that the Jewish community has yet to experience. After all, is there anyone who does not want to increase their personal happiness and life satisfaction?

The focus will be on authentic traditions, customs, practices, and teachings in a way that creates positive community. This translates into teaching people the Jewish way to happiness and well-being by developing people's character strengths and making every message relevant to their real lives, while simultaneously putting these ideals at the center of how our communities teach Torah, guide prayer, and support humanity.

I'm confident the result will be thriving and flourishing individuals and communities that care about each other and are invested in the well-being of their community. They will be concerned about happiness and positivity on a global scale. Activating the virtue of loving-kindness within our communities is a marvelous place to start.

JEWISH WELL-BEING PRACTICE
Actively Participate in Community

Jewish living is a group experience. Historically, there have been three structures within the Jewish community: the synagogue, *beit t'filah*, served as the house of prayer; the school, *beit sefer*, served as the house of learning; and the gathering center, *beit knesset*, served as the house of meeting. Each exists for the social good and to teach, practice, and expand loving-kindness for individuals, families, and communities.

Actively participating in a community that feels consistent with your interests and values can be very rewarding. If you're already connected to a community that meets your needs, consider ways to get even more involved. You'll find that the more you put in to it, the more you get out of it, as you discover new friendships, explore new interests, and express your values through meaningful activities.

If you don't belong to a Jewish community, or you're in search of a new place, try tagging along with a friend or exploring affinity groups (such as book clubs) on the web until you find a community that elevates your well-being and happiness and where your participation contributes to the strength of your community.

For Personal Reflection

1. How are you contributing to activating loving-kindness in your-self and your community?

2. What is the obligation that a religious community has to you and your family? Similarly, what obligation do you feel you have to your religious community?

3. How does your participation in a religious community elevate your well-being?

6

"If you eat the fruit of the labor of your hands, you will be happy and prosperous."

—PSALM 128:2

Work: Make Your Calling Your Career

Jewish wisdom teaches that a person's work has to be beneficial to society. One who earns his living by following an occupation which makes no constructive contribution to the well-being of others is declared by the sages to be so unreliable that he is disqualified from acting as a witness in a court of law.[98]

Modern research on job satisfaction and purpose supports this ancient teaching and concludes that "people with high well-being wake up every morning with something to look forward to doing that day." They have opportunities to do things that fit their strengths and interests. They have a deep purpose in life and a plan to attain their goals.[99]

Despite this, the American Psychological Association reports that more than ever before, today's workforce is the most unsatisfied and unhappy in their current work situation.[100] How can we help people make decisions about their life that feed their work and career goals? How can we guide them to identify what will give them a genuine sense of accomplishment (the A in the PERMA framework) and purpose?

Money Is Not the Reward; the Reward Is Meaning: Meet Isabel

Isabel, an artistic young adult in my congregation, showed great talent for creative writing and literature. Once she entered college, however, her father insisted she study business so she could join him to work in the family business.

In college, Isabel took the minimum number of business classes to graduate, while filling her schedule with comparative literature, art history, and world religion courses. Upon graduation, she began an accounting job at the family business. Her father was proud of Isabel, often introducing her as the heir to the company.

After only a few months, Isabel started getting headaches. She awoke most mornings with a stomachache and dreaded going to work. Often anxious, she felt paralyzed when asked to make a decision at the office. At the same time, she and her father were constantly fighting, so she avoided him as much as possible.

Isabel decided to see a psychologist, who listened to her with interest. She told him about her problems at work, her anxieties, and the pressure she felt from her father to take over the company. Being an only child, she was devoted to her father and felt an obligation to carry forth the company that he had started.

The psychologist understood the dilemma and believed it had to do with unresolved conflict with her father. He encouraged her to revisit her past, believing this would allow her to function better at work and be less distracted by her emotional problems.

Knowing that Isabel came from a practicing Jewish home, he reminded her of the biblical commandment to "honor your father and your mother."[101]

Isabel listened to and worked with the therapist for a few months, but her anxieties only got worse and the conflict between her and her father did not improve. Feeling stuck, she stopped going to therapy.

Being resourceful, however, Isabel tried another path. She found a life coach who specialized in helping people discover their career paths. Once again, Isabel described her situation and her desire to resolve the conflict she was having with her father, which was impacting her health, his health, and the stability of the family.

The life coach saw Isabel's problem not as unresolved anger toward her father, but rather her father's pressuring her to do what he wanted. The life coach suggested that her issues stemmed from her inability to assert herself sufficiently, combined with her inner fear of following her own desires and living independent of her father. The life coach explained that Isabel might feel better when she was no longer afraid of her father and his possessiveness.

Like Isabel and her family, this coach was also familiar with Judaism and recounted the story of young Abram in the Bible. Before he was to find his own direction in life, Abram first needed to break free and go forth from his father's house, his father's land, the land of his birth, to a new land. And there he started a new life and found great reward.

The story of Abram demonstrates a different approach to Isabel's self-realization. The coach believed that Isabel's anger was misdirected. It was not anger at her father, but anger at herself for not yet having the strength to follow her heart. Finding her own voice would give her the freedom to resolve her anxieties. She needed to take full responsibility for her life, and from that place, she would find her own well-being and life satisfaction.

Ultimately, Isabel was able to have honest conversations with herself and her father. She helped him understand what was important to her. As a result, she helped herself find her own path. She is now an editor at a small children's book publisher. While this is not a pursuit that will bring her great wealth, it will bring her great riches in the form of greater meaning, happiness, and well-being in her life.

Discovering the Life That Wants to Live in You

Isabel is not alone. A study conducted by UCLA called "The American Freshman" asked a random two hundred thousand freshman university students about their life goals. Seventy-seven percent of them responded that making money was their most important goal.[102] However, because there is only a slight relationship between wealth and happiness, having the singular goal of making money can ironically lead to unhappiness. The purpose of living a positive Jewish life is not about making money; it is about creating meaning and a true sense of accomplishment.

Yet, the state of work life in the twenty-first century paints a very different picture of what is important to people and whether they view their work as a contribution to the well-being of others. In 2017, a study showed that 50 percent of people were satisfied with their jobs, compared to 1987, when 61 percent were satisfied with their work.[103] Why are people becoming less and less satisfied with their work?

Psychologist Abraham Maslow said, "The most beautiful fate, the most wonderful good fortune that can happen to any human being, is to be paid for doing that which he passionately loves to do."[104] While it may be unrealistic to imagine that we can always be happy with our work lives, with 50 percent reporting dissatisfaction, half of us are spending too much of our time unhappy at work. As we have learned, work is one of the five areas of well-being, and when our work is unfulfilling and/or making us unhappy, it likely has a negative effect on all the key areas of our lives.

How many of those unhappy at work could benefit from following a different approach to job and career decisions? Rather than having the singular goal of making money, would greater fulfillment come from doing something that is beneficial to society? Have you ever considered making decisions about your career based on contributing to the well-being of others?

This is not to suggest one needs to drop everything and go work at a charitable organization. The value is found not by searching out the neediest and working in that setting, but by identifying the work that inspires you and answers the question "What is going to make me most fulfilled in my life, rather than what is going to make me the most money?"

For those who are unsatisfied at work, changing jobs could be a solution, but perhaps it's not the current job that is the problem. Perhaps we need to embrace the question posed by educator and activist Parker Palmer: "Is the life you are living the life that wants to live in you?"[105] In other words, have you discovered your unique gift, your highest purpose? Only you know what it may be and how to reveal it to yourself and to the world. People with the highest levels of well-being and happiness have found the life that wants to live in them. They have discovered how to align their work life with their life's calling and thereby made their calling their career.

Plant the Seeds of Your Legacy

The Jewish ideal of a person's work being a legacy to the world is best illustrated by the Talmudic tale of an old man who was planting trees.

Asked by a passerby, "Why do you plant the trees, since you will never enjoy the fruit?" the old man replied, "I found trees planted by my ancestors from which I enjoyed the fruit. Surely, it is my duty to plant trees that those who come after me might enjoy their fruit."[106] This attitude creates positive ripples from one generation to the next and teaches the important lesson of stewardship.

There comes a time in everyone's life when they need to give serious thought to the type of work they will do. For many, this happens toward the end of college and into their twenties. I encourage young people to discover themselves and the world, travel for adventure and exploration, meet people and make new friends, try different jobs, and resist the temptation to lock into a narrow career pathway too early.

The late teens and early twenties are a precious time in life, a time of freedom and self-discovery. People who take this time to explore the world and themselves end up making more self-aware decisions about their career. Self-discovery allows a person to develop their own wisdom, which is a virtue and a character strength.

Chochmah, the Hebrew word for "wisdom," is a virtue that leads to well-being. The Book of Proverbs teaches that the goal is "for learning wisdom and discipline; for understanding words of discernment; for

> **JEWISH HAPPINESS VIRTUE**
> **WISDOM**
> Wisdom, *chochmah*, is gaining knowledge from experience and developing good judgment.

acquiring the discipline for success, righteousness, justice, and equity."[107] Wisdom is gaining knowledge from experience and developing good judgment. Activating our natural wisdom through life experiences and gaining new insights will help us make important decisions about our lives that lead to positive outcomes.

In my own case, the path I took to find the life that wants to live in me was circuitous, to say the least. As the oldest child and first grandchild, I had unique expectations placed on me by parents and family to make sure that I became "successful."

My father ran a neighborhood dental practice for forty years and was beloved by his patients. I was often told that I would make a fine dentist and that I should take over my dad's business, but I was not drawn to dentistry. It did not fit my personality type nor my signature character strengths. I remember having the conversation with my dad, who said, "If you want to become a dentist, of course, the practice will be yours, but I think you have a different life living in you."

When I graduated from college, my parents encouraged me to explore business or law schools. I knew they were concerned about my future and wanted me to have a plan.

But I did have a plan. My plan was to have no official plan. My parents, however, had a different plan: I needed to start supporting myself.

While packing my belongings after graduation, my sister, Robin, called me from the summer camp where she was working. The next thing I knew, I had accepted a job as a summer camp counselor, a decision that changed my life. In 1994, at Camp Swig in Northern California, I began to discover the life that wanted to live in me.

"That Is Not a Plan; That Is Avoiding a Plan"

My family is not particularly religious, and I don't have any relatives who are rabbis. Yet in 1994 at Camp Swig, I met a handful of people my age who were on the path to become rabbis. So, it was not surprising that at the end of the summer, a spark went off in me. I had The Plan!

When I got home, we sat down for dinner, and my parents began the interrogation. "So, how was the summer? Fun? Did you hear about your high school friend, Carolyn? She got a job offer as a business consultant. You should call her. She could help you with your résumé."

"Actually, Mom and Dad, I have a plan. I'm going to take the old Volvo and go on a road trip and then travel around." Blank stares. Then my mom said, "That's not a plan. That is avoiding a plan."

My plan was to travel for as long as my summer camp earnings would allow. I would eventually apply to seminary, but becoming a rabbi was a big life decision that I was not yet ready to make. So, I took off. My grand plan lasted about three years. I worked summers at camp, made some money, and in the fall resumed my adventures. I traveled all over: Europe, Israel, Nepal, Thailand, and the United States.

On a trip back home in 1997, I went to visit my rabbi, the late Rabbi Mark Miller. I told him about my travels and my desire to become a rabbi. I explained that my parents wanted me to follow a more traditional path and had talked me into taking a prep course for the Law School Admission Test (LSAT), which seemed like the responsible thing to do.

Rabbi Miller listened and then told me a story: "This is the tale of Chayim of Volozhin. He was not a very good student during his youth. One day he told his parents that he was done with studying and wanted to attend a trade school. They agreed, but later that night, young Chayim had a dream. In this dream, an angel showed him a large pile of important books. He asked the angel, 'Whose books are those?' 'Yours,' said the angel, 'if you will have the courage to write them.'"

Story complete, he clasped his hands on his big oak desk, looked at me, smiled, and said, "Darren, be wise and be well."

Two weeks later, while taking the LSAT exam, I turned over the first exam booklet and read, "If you do not wish for this exam to count toward your permanent record, sign the bottom of the booklet, give it to the proctor, and leave the room quietly." That's exactly what I did.

The next morning, I drove to the Los Angeles campus of Hebrew Union College–Jewish Institute of Religion and applied to rabbinical school.

When I told my parents about my decision, my father said, "Darren, being a rabbi is nothing that I would ever want for myself. But knowing you and your interests, I think it is a wonderful choice." As they hugged me, I could sense their relief, especially when my mother said, "Well, at least you have a plan."

JEWISH WELL-BEING PRACTICE
Learn and Study

To learn and to study, *la'asok b'divrei Torah*, is an important Jewish practice that develops wisdom, insight, and curiosity about the world. In the words of King Solomon, "Let the wise listen and add to their learning, and let the discerning get guidance."[108]

Acquiring a heart of wisdom is the result of learning, studying, reading, meeting new people, and exploring the self and the world. There are many avenues for learning and expanding the mind, such as attending lectures at local museums or colleges, participating in book clubs at local community centers and libraries, and exploring web-based learning options available online.

Proverbs teaches, "He who acquires wisdom is his own best friend; he preserves understanding and attains happiness."[109] The Jewish people are known as "the people of the Book," and reading, along with travel, music, art, and culture, develops the heart and the mind.

For Personal Reflection

1. How do you engage in the process of finding your calling, the life that wants to live in you?

2. What personal wisdom do you believe can be gleaned from studying ancient teachings?

3. Jews are known as the people of the Book. How does book learning fit into your practice for developing wisdom?

7

"Who is rich? One who is happy with what he has."

—BEN ZOMA (SECOND-CENTURY SAGE), PIRKEI AVOT 4:1

Money: Earn It Well, Spend It Wisely

Some one thousand years ago, Rabbi Yehudah Halevi wrote, "It is a mitzvah to be happy with what we have in life."[110] Both modern science and ancient wisdom suggest that the search for money in itself does not bring happiness, but rather that *money can be spent* in the search for happiness by giving charity and creating positive life experiences.

Studies show that "people with high financial well-being manage their personal finances well and spend their money wisely. They buy experiences instead of just material possessions. They give to others instead of always spending on themselves. At a basic level, they are satisfied with their overall standard of living."[111]

Yet we seem to live in a culture where most believe (incorrectly) that more is better and that more money brings greater happiness. How can we teach people to use their money in ways that will increase their happiness and well-being? We guide people to spend their money in three ways: to become wise, to give charity, and to create positive life experiences that add meaning (the M in the PERMA framework) to a person's life.

Learning the Value of Money: Meet Carol and Lucas

Carol and her son Lucas were meeting with me to discuss his upcoming bar mitzvah ceremony and celebration. As soon as they walked into my office, I could tell something was up.

Carol began, "We are excited about Lucas's bar mitzvah, but over the weekend we hit a little bump."

"It was bigger than a little bump, Rabbi. We hit a wall," countered Lucas. "I want to have a big party and invite all my friends from school, camp, and my basketball team, and she won't let me. It's my bar mitzvah, but my parents think it's theirs."

The power struggle between kids and parents around bar or bat mitzvah time is real. Family expectations, obligations, dysfunction, hormones, and social pressures all collide in this moment.

When asked what the bar mitzvah means to him, Lucas explained that his parents made him go to Hebrew school. His family doesn't do anything Jewish at home except Hanukkah and Passover. Essentially, this was a chance for him to get a lot of gift money.

Carol answered very differently and said that everyone in her family has had a bar or bat mitzvah, but they did not grow up like Lucas and all his friends—with a lot of stuff. They view this ceremony as an important opportunity for Lucas to learn about their family values, not just to get gifts of money and throw a big party for his friends.

"Lucas, when Grandpa had his bar mitzvah, he read a passage from the Torah, everyone said 'mazel tov,' and then they enjoyed cakes and pies in the temple lobby. Very humble. Money is not where we come from. Somehow you've gotten really confused about all this."

She reminded him of the mitzvah project, a good-deeds activity, where he could demonstrate that a central part of being a Jewish adult is to help others in need.

A pillar of living a Jewish life is caring for the less fortunate. It is an expression of *tikun olam*, working to make the world better for everyone, and the coming-of-age moment should be linked to this virtue so that children learn how to give from their hearts in order to receive the most fulfilling reward: the feeling of creating positivity in the world.

One of the differences between acting like a child and acting like an adult is that a child is often allowed to think only about their needs, while an adult is called to support the needs of others. A mature person takes responsibility for working toward a just and fair world. It's the idea of paying it forward, doing something nice for the next person because you know what it is like to have nice things done for you.

Lucas apparently absorbed the lessons his mother and I were trying to teach him. While I imagined he was trying to find an angle to negotiate the party, instead he surprised me by saying, "Okay, Rabbi. I get it. It's not all about the money and party. I'll do a mitzvah project by working some shifts at our local food pantry on the weekends and give them 10 percent of my gift money as well."

Learning the value of money comes at a price. In the world we live in today, it can be difficult to teach young people that the pursuit of money in itself does not bring happiness, but rather the opportunity comes with how money is used, which can raise happiness. For so many children growing up today in our highly materialistic world, learning this lesson on the eve of adulthood can be one of our greatest gifts to their future, and ours.

Can Money Create Happiness? Yes, It Can

Many people mistakenly believe that more money translates to more happiness. However, research shows that increased wealth often fails to provide as much happiness as many people expect.[112] In the words of Ecclesiastes, "A lover of money never has his fill of money, nor a lover of wealth his fill of income."[113]

Yet we know that the realities of life demand money. A widely cited study by Daniel Kahneman and Angus Deaton in 2010 showed that in the United States, for single-person households that earned approximately $75,000 per year (adjusted for cost of living), making additional money had no significant impact on their day-to-day feelings of happiness.[114] Once a person can pay for daily necessities and comforts like food, housing, and basic health care, seeking greater income can even be detrimental to well-being.[115]

The desire for unneeded money takes people's time and energy away from activities that have been shown to increase happiness, like investing in relationships, community, and health. Further, if the perceived need for more money is driven by a desire for social prestige—an effort to keep up appearances or project an image of success—this actively detracts from well-being. The irony is that earning and spending money from a place of inadequacy, jealousy, or comparison with one's neighbor can feed negative emotions that undermine happiness.

As the Jewish sages teach, "Whoever seeks more than he needs hinders himself from enjoying what he has."[116] But if we know that wealth and happiness have little do with each other after a certain threshold, can we use the power of the money we do have to increase our life satisfaction and make a positive impact? The answer is yes.

Money can be a tool for increasing happiness when it is spent in the service of our genuine well-being. In this spirit, let's consider a Jewish framework for thinking about the role of money in our lives. We will call one aspect of money *shekels* and the other *gelt*. The money that we use to pay bills and support basic needs (like food, rent, heath care, and clothing) we will call *shekels*, like the currency of the State of Israel and the biblical term for money.

The second aspect of money we'll call *gelt*, like the coins used to play the dreidel game during Hanukkah. *Gelt* is a sixteenth-century Yiddish word related to the Old English *gelde*, which referred to a type of payment. For our purposes, let's think of *gelt* as the money we spend to elevate our well-being in three specific ways: to become wise, to give charity, and to create positive life experiences.[117]

Spend Money to Become Wise

The Jewish sage Solomon ibn Gabirol was asked by a student, "Who do you believe are greater? The wise or the rich?" "The wise," he answered. The student continued, "But if that is the case, why do you find more of the wise at the doors of the wealthy than the wealthy at the doors of the wise?" The sage responded, "Because the wise appreciate the value of riches, but the rich do not similarly appreciate the value of wisdom."[118]

How do we use money to become wise? We spend it on enrichment classes, lectures, books, theater, movies, trips, and social time with friends and family. We effectively become wise by engaging in activities that expand our life experiences, boost our happy moods, increase our optimistic thoughts, and help us grow interpersonally.[119]

Give Money to Charity

The second way to increase our happiness through money is by spending on other people.[120] The 2006–2008 Gallup World Happiness Survey asked over two hundred thousand people in 136 countries about what makes them happy. One question compared whether people had donated to charity in the past month with their current state of life satisfaction.[121] Overwhelmingly, people who had donated reported greater satisfaction with life—this was true for poor and rich countries alike.[122]

A central pillar of Jewish living is giving tzedakah, charity. The Torah teaches, "Do not harden your heart and shut your hand against your needy kinsman. Rather, you must open your hand and lend him sufficient for whatever he needs."[123] Tzedakah is like tithing, the biblical command to give 10 percent of one's earnings as charity. Even a homeless person is required to give tzedakah, according to Jewish law,[124] because giving charity boosts happiness and teaches humility.

The word tzedakah is closely related to the Hebrew word tzedek, which means "justice." Justice draws on strengths that support connections to community, such as teamwork, fairness, and leadership. When

> **JEWISH HAPPINESS VIRTUE**
> **JUSTICE**
> Justice, tzedek, is behavior that is fair and reasonable. It draws on strengths that support connections to community, such as teamwork, fairness, and leadership.

we act with a sense of *tzedek*, we treat and support people the same and give everyone an equal chance. When actualized, the virtue of justice, *tzedek*, increases well-being and happiness.

When we seek ways to activate *tzedek*, justice, we participate in building a fairer and more balanced world. If we believe that we are all in this together, then charity, tzedakah, helps create a more just world for all.

Spend Money to Create Positive Experiences

We all have different interests and personality styles. The experiences that bring me happiness, like travel and discovering new places with my family, may be different from what brings you happiness. You may like writing poetry, playing music, relaxing on beaches, or seeing famous works of art—there are endless examples. But whatever the experiences are, we can spend *gelt* to create happy moments and positive memories by becoming "time affluent." You have heard the phrase "Time is money." Instead of thinking that time should be spent on making money, let's think about how to spend money on creating time for living well.

Spending time traveling brings me real happiness. Over one holiday break during my seminary studies in Israel, a group of friends and I traveled to the Sinai Peninsula in Egypt to spend eight days walking in the desert. We were interested in seeing firsthand where the oldest stories of the Bible came from and to imagine how the desert environment may have shaped the mind-set of the ancient Israelites.

The final two days were spent at Santa Caterina, a fourth-century monastery at the foot of Jabal Musa, Arabic for "Mountain of Moses," thought by some to be the biblical Mount Sinai. We woke up on the last day of our trip to hike to the top of Jabal Musa to watch the sunrise and to visit the shrine dedicated to God's giving the Ten Commandments to Moses.

This was a remarkable trip, and though it was years ago, I still remember the faces of my friends as we ascended the mountain, the emotions of arriving at the top and watching the sun emerge over the Jordan Valley, and feeling deeply inspired and intellectually curious.

We each recall that experience as a highlight of our lives, and whenever we see each other, we're bound to refer to something that happened on that trip. Over the years, I have told others about that journey and shared the photos with countless people. While I cannot remember how much the trip cost in terms of money, whatever it did cost, the *gelt* led to an experience that has added to the richness of my life. To this day, I cherish those memories.

JEWISH WELL-BEING PRACTICE
Give Charity

Tzedek refers to the religious obligation to do what is fair, right, and just. Giving charity, tzedakah, is an expression of working to form a more just world. Unlike voluntary charity, Jewish tradition teaches that tzedakah is a religious obligation that must be performed regardless of one's financial standing. It is taught that tzedakah (we have described it as *gelt*) does not actually belong to the donor. Rather, tzedakah belongs to God, who merely entrusts it with humanity so that we may use it properly for those deserving of it.[125] We can think of tzedakah as the vehicle that regulates justice and fairness in the world.

Throughout the year, there are special days to give tzedakah. During the High Holy Days, it is believed that giving tzedakah helps us to be sealed in the Book of Life. On Passover, tzedakah is given to those in need, so all will be able to eat a Passover meal. And on Purim, it is customary to give food and tzedakah to at least two poor people in order to increase total happiness on earth during the Hebrew month of Adar.

Maimonides ranks eight levels of giving tzedakah (with 1 being the highest), each designed to make our world more just and more fair for all of humanity:

1. Giving an interest-free loan to a person in need, forming a partnership with a person in need, giving a grant to a person in need, or finding a job for a person in need, so long as that loan, grant, partnership, or job results in the person no longer living by relying upon others

2. Giving anonymously to an unknown recipient via a person (or public fund) who is trustworthy, wise, and can perform acts of tzedakah with your money in a most impeccable fashion

3. Giving anonymously to a known recipient

4. Giving publicly to an unknown recipient

5. Giving before being asked

6. Giving adequately after being asked

7. Giving willingly, but inadequately

8. Giving out of pity or unwillingly

For Personal Reflection

1. In what ways do you spend money to increase your own well-being and happiness?

2. How are you using money to create a more fair, just, and positive world?

3. If you could increase your charitable giving to create more justice in the world, where would you elect to give more?

Part Three

Activating Positive Judaism When Living Hurts

> "You cannot control what happens to you in life, but you can always control what you will feel about what happens to you."
>
> —Viktor Frankl (Holocaust survivor)

We have explored Jewish ways to thrive in the five areas of life: relationships, health, community, work, and money. We now explore the other side of each area, when life is a struggle or when living hurts. The next five chapters are designed to help us prepare, heal, and renew our life when forces beyond our control send us unwelcome challenges.

In the face of misfortune, my grandmother was famous for repeating the Jewish proverb, "This too shall pass." I found comfort in these words. In addition, as a person who has faced personal challenges and as a rabbi who has witnessed the trials of others, I have learned that Judaism offers a treasury of wisdom and insight that is even more supportive and practical than "This too shall pass."

Nobody gets through life without some pain. While people may face similar life events, each is unique and personal. We all find ourselves struggling at times, yet each person experiences pain and loss differently, sometimes in lonely and confusing ways.

The next chapters offer an approach to facing a sampling of life's challenges by activating the teachings of Positive Judaism. Here in Part Three, we will:

- Explore the five areas of well-being from their other side [broken relationships, illness, isolation, job loss, and money problems].
- Study five virtues: forgiveness, courage, spirituality, gratitude, and perseverance.
- See how these strengths are taught and deepened through the observance of Yom Kippur, visiting the sick, observing Passover, volunteering, and meditation.

These virtues and practices are central to personal transformation and change, and we will view them from a Jewish perspective. Similarly, we will see that these same virtues and practices have been shown to support growth and healing. While you may be thinking that some of the chapters ahead may not apply to you, never forget that Noah was called to build the ark before the storm. Preparing ourselves by knowing and/or strengthening specific virtues and practices to help cope with life's inevitable challenges can help us to face future ordeals, reflect with new perspective on previous incidents, and learn strategies to help ourselves and others face hardships.

8

"No person should be expected to dwell in the same den with a serpent."

—Babylonian Talmud, Y'vamot 112b

When Relationships Fall Apart: Broken Bonds, Separation, and Divorce

If healthy relationships are a key factor of happiness and well-being, what can be done when our relationships become strained? At some point in the course of life, most people will find that a relationship has faltered. The bonds between friends, parents and children, siblings, significant others, committed partners, spouses, neighbors, and coworkers all have the potential for unique sets of problems.

Divorce and marital separation are at record highs, and nearly one-half of all marriages end in divorce, leaving many people affected (parents, children, friends, and colleagues). Let us recall the story of the craftsman in chapter 3 who turned the king's cracked diamond into a rose and made it more beautiful than he ever imagined. Even so, not all relationships are destined to last a lifetime. Regardless of the circumstances that lead to divorce, once the decision is made to move apart, there is a pathway for positive healing and reconciliation, which we will explore in this chapter.

When Relationships Fall Apart: Meet Elizabeth and Michael

Elizabeth and Michael had been married eight years when I met with them to discuss their marriage difficulties. Two successful professionals, they had met in London in their thirties, fallen in love quickly, and gotten married within a year. Soon after their wedding, Elizabeth got pregnant with their daughter, and they returned to New York City.

When they arrived at my office, they could barely look at each other. She complained about his long work hours. He complained that she did not respect or understand the importance of his working hard now so that they would not have to worry about money in the future.

She felt that he was sacrificing marriage and fatherhood to his career. He was bitter that she was always tired after working and managing their daughter's activities, and she never wanted to be physically close. He felt rejected. She fell asleep alone. They fought about everything.

Michael and Elizabeth were in a lot of pain. I suggested they take one night each week for a special date and plan a weekend away every few months. I encouraged them to share a meal together as a family on Shabbat and be present with each other—without computers, phones, or work—to focus on their family relationship.

They had agreed to give it a try, but it was not working. In fact, it was making things worse. Since they were spending more time together, there was more conflict. Elizabeth told me, "It's all so forced, nothing genuine. Aside from our daughter, we have so little in common. Whenever we're alone it's even more painful, because neither of us wants to be there."

And right there and then, she called it. "Michael, it's time. I want a divorce." Immediately sitting taller, with a huge emotional burden lifted, she was ready to take responsibility and control of her well-being and happiness. Within a month, Michael moved into his own place, and their daughter Melody started going back and forth between her parents' homes.

While some may view any decision to end a marriage with disdain, for many couples there comes a moment when they know it's time to move apart. It is better to break up with integrity and courage when it's clear the marriage is wrong, especially when children are involved, than to stay together working on a relationship that cannot be fixed.

In some divorces, there is drama—affairs, abuse, neglect, and so on. Too often divorced couples become bitter and angry, and the negative emotions are highly toxic to everyone around them. I did not sense that would be the case with Michael and Elizabeth, but they still had a lot to figure out about how to move forward.

When they came to see me, we talked about what a positive outcome to their divorce would look like. How they could uncouple in the healthiest way for themselves and their daughter? Which character strengths would they draw upon to pass through this chapter and still grow as people?

They created a co-parenting plan, agreeing to never say anything negative about one another when Melody was around and to give her full access to each parent no matter their custody schedule. Melody had the option to come and go freely between them. They agreed never to put her in the middle of their conflict and that they would share birthday parties, graduations, life ceremonies, holiday dinners, and family activities together.

Fast-forward: Melody is a well-adjusted teenager, flourishing in school and a leader on her travel volleyball team. Elizabeth remarried, to a man who was also divorced with children, and together they've built a family that is a much better fit for her and her new husband. Michael is single, thriving in his career, and ascending the ladder at his firm.

For Elizabeth and Michael, divorce was a mitzvah, a positive step in all their lives, and everyone is healthier and happier.

In Certain Situations, Divorce Is a Mitzvah

I am not a proponent of divorce. I am an advocate for positive marriages and unified families. I pray for *shalom bayit*, peace in the home, because the family is the foundation of community and society, and research shows that people in healthy marriages are happier than those who are divorced.[126]

When I stand with a couple under their wedding canopy, the overwhelming feelings in the room are for love, hope, and future. A marriage may be full of promise, but the couple may not be one another's *bashert*, the partner they are destined for in life.

Divorce can be painful, confusing, and sad. On the other hand, it can also be freeing and a new beginning. I have seen divorce ruin people, forever sour their lives, char them with resentment, and destroy them spiritually. However, there is another way forward for the millions of divorced couples and families—the positive divorce. A positive divorce depends in most situations on each partner's ability to forgive. Having lived through the experience, I can say with conviction that a positive divorce is a mitzvah.

No matter how strong you are at the start of your separation or at the legal end of your divorce, the process is painful. The rupture of divorce ripples through all the relationships of the previously married couple, so that living through a divorce can feel like being on a boat in rough seas. Sleepless nights. Financial uncertainty. Anxiety about children's mental health. Social stigma. But eventually, the seas calm and people can begin to imagine a positive new future.

The good news is that most people bounce back from their divorces stronger than before. The overwhelming research on the effects that divorce has on individuals is that on average, the happiness levels of people who divorce increase over time.[127] People are resilient, and when they have the desire to turn their traumatic life experiences into growth opportunities, they will thrive. The same is true for children.

The Facts on Divorce and Children

Most parents would do anything to protect their children. In fact, several studies show that kids are the reason that many unhappy couples stay together.[128] Still, most of the research on children of divorce demonstrates that considering the totality of a child's life experience, the long-term effects of divorce are often not as great as parents fear.

At first glance, it appears that children of divorce have a higher propensity toward unhappiness and depression. They are often sadder and act out more in the classroom. They have lower levels of confidence and self-esteem and more health problems, making depression even more likely.[129] However, these issues may not be the result of their parents' divorce, but something much more significant. The issues may be the result of their parents' low level of well-being, poor life satisfaction, and unhappiness.

To get to the heart of the matter, we must go deeper and compare the effects on children who live in a home where there is significant parental conflict to how well children fare after divorce. The findings are clear: children exposed to major parental conflict suffer from depression, anxiety, and have troubled relationships with their peers at much higher rates than children of divorced parents.[130] In other words, marital conflict is worse on children than is divorce.

Parental happiness and well-being are critical for their own lives and for the sake of their children's lives. One study showed that a troubled marriage presents as big a risk factor for heart disease as a regular smoking habit.[131] The bottom line is that what is in children's best interest, always, is the well-being of their parents.

The Talmud recounts a story of a Rabbi Yossi who was once married to a woman who would insult him in public, even in the presence of his students. When his student Elazar urged him to divorce her, Rabbi Yossi said that he would like to but lacked the funds to pay for the divorce. So, the student raised the funds to enable him to buy his way out of the marriage.

His now ex-wife then married another man, who subsequently lost all his money and became blind. His wife had no other option but to lead him around begging for charity. One time, nobody in the city gave them anything. Her husband asked her, "Is there another neighborhood in the city where we can go?" She replied, "There is one other neighborhood, but my first husband lives there, and I am too embarrassed to go there." Just then, Rabbi Yossi saw the couple walk past. He saw their poor state and provided them with a house and food for the rest of their lives.[132]

In this story, forgiveness and compassion take center stage. Though

Rabbi Yossi and his ex-wife were not each other's *bashert*, were not destined to be with each other, they had been married and loved one another for a chapter of their lives. Rabbi Yossi came to support his ex-spouse because he could. I imagine that Rabbi Yossi needed to forgive his ex-wife for the public humiliation and insults, and needed to forgive himself and take his own measure of responsibility for their divorce.

Maimonides wrote, "When asked by an offender for forgiveness, one should forgive with a sincere mind and a willing spirit. . . . Forgiveness is natural to the seed of Israel."[133] In my experience, forgiveness has been one of the important strengths that has allowed former partners to move forward in their lives.

Forgiving Is Something We Do for Ourselves

The ability to forgive, *s'lichah* in Hebrew, is a character strength, but forgiveness can be hard. It's the ability to find compassion and give up feelings of resentment toward anyone who has hurt us. It is also a deep understanding that people change, and others must accept that change. But to be clear, forgiving others is something that we do for ourselves. Research concludes that forgiveness helps people be less anxious, less angry, and less bitter.[134] In the words of philosopher Hannah Arendt, "Forgiveness is the key to action and freedom."[135]

The responsibility to forgive is your own. Previously married people and their families can choose to carry the burdens of a difficult divorce or grow to forgive and move on to positively embrace the full expression of a new chapter in life. We cannot foretell the future, nor can we change the past, but we can take positive action today to improve our well-being. In this regard, the biblical story of Joseph provides an excellent example of the virtue of forgiveness.

The youngest brother of twelve siblings, Joseph was sold into slavery by his brothers, because they were jealous of him. But Joseph was resilient and creative and impressed his captors, his fellow slaves, and even the Pharaoh with his ability to interpret dreams. He even received many promotions over the years and eventually earned a leadership position in the Pharaoh's court.

At one point, during a famine in Israel, Joseph's brothers traveled to Egypt to appeal at Pharaoh's court for food and supplies. Little did they know, since they could not recognize him in his fine clothing, that they were appealing to their brother Joseph, the one they had sold into slavery.

Joseph listened, and then in a highly emotional reveal, he told his brothers the truth. Imagine the shock when he said to them, "Now, do not be distressed or reproach yourselves because you sold me [into slavery]. . . . God has sent me ahead of you to ensure your survival on earth, and to save your lives in an extraordinary deliverance. So, it was not you who sent me here, but God."[136]

This is forgiveness. We may have expected Joseph to want revenge after feeling hurt or betrayed, but we must draw on our character strengths to resist vengeance. We cannot know the future, but by living our best lives and forgiving when we have the opportunity, our lives will improve, and we will once again be in a place to help others and to have a positive impact on the ones we love most.

Applying Character Strengths During a Divorce

Every divorce is different, and depending on the circumstances, individuals will need to draw on a variety of character strengths to guide their way to healing. In my own divorce, learning to forgive has been the most important element of my process, keeping in mind that forgiveness is at the bottom of my list of strengths.

My ex-wife and I were married for eleven years before we separated. We both admit we waited too long. It took my near-death car accident to act on what we knew was true: despite our best efforts to make things right, we were both unhappy in our marriage.

My brush with death taught me that I was no longer willing to carry the burden. The fears that I had about divorce, the potential effect on our children, and the impact on my career were real and heavy. They constrained me. Despite having taught lessons about facing fears and personal transformation, I could not force my life. Life has its own timeline and is only ready when it's ready.

At last, when my life was ready for this change, three teachings from Rabbi Nachman of Breslov (nineteenth century) profoundly supported and sustained me:

1. "If you believe breaking is possible, believe fixing is possible."

2. "The world is a narrow bridge; the most important thing is not to be overwhelmed by fear."

3. "Always remember happiness is not a side matter in your spiritual journey. It is essential."

My ex-wife and I had different experiences of our divorce, and our pathways for coping and recovery were and continue to be different. She draws upon her strengths of perseverance, zest, and social intelligence to navigate the issues of our uncoupling. My signature strengths of creativity, curiosity, and resilience bolster me. Being mindful of our strengths enables us to separate, together, especially during the most challenging and confusing moments. Divorce is a process, not an event. Thankfully, we can both honestly say that for us and for our children, we're all better off.

Many people facing the prospect of divorce eventually decide to end their marriage. Others know someone close to them who is struggling to determine if it is time to go. Only those involved can know when the time is right. Nevertheless, it is important to know what the studies conclude: people in unhappy marriages and their children generally become happier and healthier after divorce,[137] and your personal well-being is the most important factor in your life and the lives of your children.

JEWISH WELL-BEING PRACTICE
Observe Yom Kippur and Forgive

During the ten days of the Jewish New Year celebrations of Rosh Hashanah and Yom Kippur, forgiveness, *s'lichah*, is encouraged as one of the central practices. It is common to spend these ten days performing acts of forgiveness to find peace and contentment at the start of a new year and to be "sealed in the Book of Life."

Yom Kippur is considered the most sacred day of the year, and we are called to say, "I hereby forgive all who have transgressed against me, whether on purpose or by accident, whether in this lifetime or on any other plane."[138] Tradition teaches that prior to the start of Yom Kippur, the following prayer for forgiveness is to be recited:

> "I know that there is no one so righteous that they have not wronged another, financially or physically, through deed or speech. This pains my heart within me, because wrongs between humans and their fellow are not atoned by Yom Kippur, until the wronged one is appeased. . . . For behold, I forgive with a final and resolved forgiveness anyone who has wronged me, whether in person or property, even if they slandered me or spread falsehoods against me. So, I release anyone who has injured me either in person or in property, or has committed any manner of sin that one may commit against another . . . I fully and finally forgive everyone."[139]

Jewish tradition places such great emphasis on forgiveness that it takes center stage on the holiest day of the year, yet one does not need to wait until Yom Kippur to practice forgiveness. Forgiveness can be a daily practice by having honest conversations with family and friends about ways you hurt one another and seeking forgiveness. Writing letters to people who may have wronged you or whom you may have wronged in some way is also a good healing technique. And finally, journaling about past events has been shown to offer relief from the burdens people carry.

For Personal Reflection

1. If you have experienced a failed relationship or divorce, what character strengths could you activate to create more positive relationships in your life going forward?

2. How can you find your way to forgiveness of yourself and others for past wrongs or mistakes?

3. Is there someone no longer living from whom you would like forgiveness? If so, how can you address that need?

9

"Had I not fallen I would have not arisen. Had I not been subject to darkness, I would not have seen the light."

—JEWISH PROVERB

When Illness Comes: Coping with Pain and Sickness

Over the course of a lifetime, everyone faces illness and pain. We know that the quality of our physical and mental health is a significant factor in how we feel on an hourly and daily basis. Yet what can we do to cope with the myriad of health issues that we and our loved ones will face over a lifetime to support our well-being and theirs?

There are transformative Jewish practices, wisdom, and insights that help us approach and understand suffering and pain. It's been shown that prayer, meditation, genuine human connections, and drawing on strengths like bravery and courage can have a very positive impact on our health during illness, treatment, and recovery.

"I Always Wanted to Do This": Meet Arnie

Attentive, intense, and focused, Arnie sat near the front of the sanctuary every year on Rosh Hashanah. As soon as the Jewish New Year service concluded, Arnie was first in line to greet me and wish me an easy fast and a good new year. For many years, that was my entire relationship with Arnie, until one day, out of the blue, he called for an appointment. There had been some changes in his life that he wanted to discuss.

Four months earlier, he had suffered a heart attack during a meeting at his law firm. Following emergency cardiac surgery, his doctors told him his heart problems were likely the result of years of stress. Arnie said, "Rabbi, my first thought in the recovery room was I'm done with all this. I've got all the money I could ever spend. I want to live, and there's so much I want to do."

With total clarity, he called his assistant from the hospital and told her to pack up his things. He was retiring. Despite insistent pleas from his partners cajoling him to take some time, reminding him that he was still in his prime, and laying on the guilt that his clients needed him, he stuck to his guns. He realized he never really knew his partners, and they didn't really know him. In fact, he felt that he didn't really know himself.

While not a religious man, Arnie respected our traditions. He reminded me of a talk I had given on PTSG: post-traumatic stress growth. Arnie felt that he was experiencing something like this and that his heart attack was the best thing that had ever happened to him.

Studies confirm Arnie's experience. Research has shown that some common responses to trauma include developing a deeper and more sophisticated philosophy of life; feeling a greater sense of compassion for others who suffer; improved relationships with real friends; and a renewed belief in the ability to endure and prevail in anything that comes our way.[140]

I shared with Arnie the Jewish insight into the meaning of the caduceus, the snake symbol on medical signs and shields. Snakes hibernate and then, just before returning to life, they shed their skin. This symbolizes an inner transformation that occurs in parallel with a physical change. It was similarly the snake, or serpent, who encouraged Adam and Eve to eat from the tree in the Garden of Eden that opened their eyes to awareness. Arnie had experienced the transformational power in his own process of shedding skin as he got nearer to the tree, a symbol of knowledge, life, and wisdom.

He thanked me and left. At the end of the summer, a postcard arrived.

"Rabbi, I'm on my own Jack Kerouac road trip enjoying the desert snakes. I always wanted to do this! I won't be seeing you this year for Yom Kippur. Have an easy fast. Happy New Year, Arnie."

Judaism on Illness, Pain, and Suffering

"Not to have pain is not to have been human," teaches an old Jewish saying. Judaism acknowledges that the human journey includes illness, pain, and suffering. Many of us know people in pain, who may be facing daily struggles with physical or mental illness or both. We, or the ones we love, may have or could develop cancer, diabetes, heart disease, addictions, or any number of physical issues. We're also experiencing new levels of mental illness today, and as a result, most of us know people who are living with schizophrenia, depression, bipolar disorder, or any of a host of other ailments.

In addition to traditional and alternative medical treatments that address illness and pain, there is a treasury of Jewish wisdom, prayer, and teachings to help reduce a person's suffering. Prayer may not be able to diminish pain, but a landmark study of forty-four thousand cancer patients revealed that regular prayer and spiritual practices increased optimism and reduced suffering.[141]

In the late 1990s, I had a part-time rotation as a chaplain at Columbia Hospital in New York. Part of my own practice of visiting patients was to enter a patient's room blindly—that is, without prior knowledge of their condition or medical situation. This allowed me to be fully present with the patient and not enter with any preconceived notions about what to say or how to behave. There is one visit I will never forget.

I entered a hospital room one morning. A man and woman in their mid-sixties were standing over a patient lying on the bed.

They looked at me confused, and as I approached the hospital bed, I saw the patient for the first time. Her skin had a greenish cast. Her body was rigid. She could not move. I later learned she had scleroderma, a chronic connective tissue disease.

Her mother turned me around, reversed me into the hallway, and closed the door. She took a deep breath, and the tears began to flow. "Father, why is God doing this to us? It's not fair. She's not ready—and neither are we. But you can pray for us."

She had assumed I was a priest there to administer the last rites to their daughter, as would be common in their faith.

"I understand. Let us pray together."

We went back into the room and held hands around the young woman's bed, while I shared a few words of prayer. As we stood there in silence, I could tell her parents were deep in prayer and meditation, and for the moment, they had found calm in prayer on their path to healing.

A Jewish Approach to Healing

There is often so much involved with illness, pain, and suffering beyond the medical issues. First, those of us who have been ill or have supported those facing disease know that it's rarely only the patient who suffers; many people are affected by the illness. Everyone involved experiences an illness, recovery, and healing in different and important ways.

Second, illness and pain can lead us to ask the big questions in life, yet we often fail to have concrete answers to so many of those questions. Why me? Why our beloved child? Why Mom? Why Dad? In these moments, it's not uncommon to bring God into the mystery of illness. "Why is God doing this to her? She does not deserve it."

In Judaism, spiritual practices are often part of the healing experience. People turn to religious rituals and faith leaders to help anchor their confusion, suffering, and fear as they work toward recovery and renewed health.

There is an ancient story about Rabbi Elazar, who had grown sick. His friend Rabbi Yochanan went to visit him and noticed that he was weeping. "Why do you weep? Did you not study enough Torah? Is it because you lacked wealth or that you have no children?" Elazar replied, "I weep because my beauty is going to rot in the earth." Yohanan replied, "For that, you surely have reason to weep." They both cried and Yohanan said, "Give me your hand." So Elazar gave his hand to Yohanan, and Elazar was healed.[142]

In Judaism, the practice of *bikur cholim*, "visiting the sick," is so important that tradition teaches that when an ill person receives a visitor, the visitor removes one-sixtieth of the person's suffering. During a visit, it is customary to say the Mi Shebeirach prayer, which states, "May the One who blessed our ancestors bring blessing and healing to all who suffer illness, and may God restore all to health and vigor, granting them physical and spiritual well-being."

Earlier, when we explored the power of prayer in chapter 4, we learned that people who pray or who have congregations that pray on their behalf are likely to have a speedier recovery than those who do not. Prayer engenders optimism, and optimism encourages improved physical health. While we may be ill, a genuine visit reaffirms our humanness and reminds us of our connection to the world outside the hospital room.

As when God visited Abraham after his circumcision, visiting the sick is considered a divine act.[143] Jewish tradition teaches that when we are ill, our visitors channel the Divine Presence, which may inspire feelings of optimism, hope, and love.

The Positive Power of Meditation on Healing

In addition to the value of a personal visit, studies confirm that meditation has the healing power to reduce suffering and even reduce the severity of an illness or disease.[144] Mindfulness programs and interventions have taught people with chronic back pain, victims of accidents, cancer patients, paraplegics, and returning soldiers how to meditate. Mindfulness meditations guide people to focus on the present moment by focusing on the breath. The idea is to cultivate attention on the body and mind as it exists in the moment and so help with pain, both physical and emotional.

Dr. Jon Kabat-Zinn, a leading expert in the science of meditation and mindfulness, teaches that meditation "often results in apprehending the constantly changing nature of sensations, even highly unpleasant ones, and thus their impermanence. It also gives rise to the direct experience that 'the pain is not me.'" As a result, some of his patients found ways to be in a different relationship with their pain, while others felt it diminish. He also discovered that people's immune functions were enhanced through mindfulness meditation.[145]

Not only can meditation improve our physical state, it has also been shown to improve our emotional state by raising our levels of happiness and positive emotions, while at the same time reducing anxiety and depression.[146]

Meditation has a long tradition in Jewish practice and derives from the notion of being present, being here now. Several times in the Torah, the word *hineini* appears, which translates to "I am here. I am present." When Abraham is called to take his son Isaac to the mountaintop, he replies, "*Hineini*, I am present."[147] At the beginning of Joseph's long journey that ends with him saving his family from starvation, he says, "*Hineini*, I am present."[148] And at the burning bush, where Moses learns of his destiny to become the leader of the Israelites, he replies, "*Hineini*, I am present."[149] *Hineini* is the biblical expression of the flow state,[150] a psychological state of being fully immersed and fully present in whatever you are doing.

Our ability to find *hineini*, to be present, no matter what we encounter in life, can have a significant influence on the healing experience. On this, I speak from personal experience, as my family was put to the test when my nephew was diagnosed with brain cancer.

Noah's Cancer

In 2016, my then ten-year-old nephew was diagnosed with a rare form of brain cancer. One day, bright, curious, and clever Noah was living an idyllic life in the suburbs of Northern California. The next day, he was admitted to Children's Hospital in Oakland for brain surgery.

How could any of us have been prepared for this shock? It was like a bomb went off in Noah's life, and ours. We were terrified.

With extraordinary medical intervention by expert doctors, nurses, and social workers, Noah survived. He is one of the lucky ones, and words cannot adequately express our gratitude for his highly skilled team of medical professionals and social workers. During the course of his long and arduous recovery, we learned some things that may be helpful to anyone facing a major, catastrophic illness.

The support from the community and Noah's school was overwhelming. An email network and blog started immediately to keep everyone connected and the channels of support open wide. On the first Friday night following surgery, more than forty of his friends and their parents took over the hospital cafeteria for a big Shabbat dinner. Fellow parents stepped up to make sure Noah's younger brothers got to school, continued their activities, and had meals every day.

For the entire year, the local synagogues had Noah's name on their Mi Shebeirach lists and would recite a prayer of healing at every gathering. The Oakland A's baseball team sent a get-well package to the hospital and invited Noah to throw out the opening pitch at his first opportunity. Ronald McDonald House sent Noah several care packages, and the Make-A-Wish Foundation sent him a voucher to travel anywhere in the world the first chance he had to get away. This all gave Noah hope and kept him focused on his future, which was a tremendous gift.

In 2018, at Noah's bar mitzvah celebration, his parents shared these words:

> Dearest Noah, as you become bar mitzvah today, you join the many generations in your family who have been called to the Torah before you. You are a link in the chain that connects your past with the future.
>
> You have endured things that most people, let alone a boy your age, will never be able to comprehend. As a result, you live every day to its fullest. You have taught us how to live with gratitude and grace. How to be a better person. How to see the good in every situation. Your perseverance, loving nature, strength, and positive attitude are infectious, and we couldn't be prouder.

There was not a dry eye in the synagogue that evening, and everyone was recalling our journey with Noah. Though he was the patient, everyone from family and friends to strangers were engaged in his treatment and recovery. The strength of their community and the depth of their relationships brought tremendous support and a reminder that life has innate meaning. Throwing the opening pitch at the Oakland A's game nourished high positive emotions. Everyone had a goal to achieve: save the life of a child.

One additional insight: In the pre-op room leading into Noah's first surgery, Noah got scared, began panicking, and started to scream and thrash around to the point that he had to be sedated. Over the course of the year, however, Noah changed. He learned how to manage his emotions, found his courage, and developed methods to resist his fear.[151] Courage was always in him, but until this ordeal, he was never challenged to activate it so specifically. The courage he discovered helped him become more emotionally resilient, and like so many survivors, cancer transformed him.

The Hebrew word for courage is *ometz lev*. *Ometz* is "strength" and *lev* is "heart," and thus, in Jewish thought, the virtue of courage is the "strength of the heart." This implies that courage is less about acts of bravery and physical might, and more about the truth of who we are inside. When we fully put our hearts into something, we activate the courage to face, and hopefully overcome, our challenges.

> **JEWISH HAPPINESS VIRTUE**
> **COURAGE**
> Courage, *ometz lev*, is the ability to face, and hopefully overcome, our challenges.

Naturally, despite its positive outcome, Noah's cancer was not a welcome life experience. He, and the entire family, would trade it back with pleasure. Nevertheless, life is precarious and can change without warning. In the words of Viktor Frankl, "Forces beyond your control can take away everything you possess except one thing: your freedom to choose how you will respond to a situation. You cannot control what happens to you in life, but you can always control what you will feel about what happens to you."[152] Noah taught all of us this lesson.

Visit the Sick

Visiting the sick, *bikur cholim*, is a central practice of Jewish living that counters two burdens of illness: isolation and lack of community. At a time of illness, a visit provides the comfort of human connection and can bolster courage, hope, and optimism. While it may feel uncomfortable or awkward to sit with someone who is ill, be strengthened to know that Jewish tradition teaches that this act "brings goodness to the world."[153]

When visiting people in the hospital, go with the purpose to elevate their mood. Treat them like a dear friend rather than a patient, act positively, and bring them good news from the outside to boost their spirits. Offer comforting attention by holding their hands and brightening their room.

Visiting the sick helps to build courage for both the visitor and the visited. Whether you are calling on friends, family, or even strangers, you will be in a setting to learn about humility and to grow in wisdom about the importance of good health and the fragility of life.

For Personal Reflection

1. Describe a time when you were visited by someone when you were sick. How did you feel just after the visit?

2. Visiting the sick may be one way to build courage. What are other experiences in your life that have expanded your strength of courage?

3. How would your days feel different if you could activate more courage in your daily life? What would change?

10

"It is not good for people to be alone."

—GENESIS 2:18

Alone in the World: Facing Loneliness and Isolation

Jewish wisdom teaches, "Get yourself a friend."[154] Friendships and authentic connections to community contribute to well-being and happiness. Yet, a well-respected study on loneliness shows that people are reporting higher levels of loneliness and isolation than ever before.[155]

The Psalmist cries out, "I am lonely and afflicted and my heart is troubled; free me from my distress."[156] The authors of the Bible had keen insight into the journey of life, for who has not felt lonely at some point in their lives? Loneliness can break the human spirit, so where can we turn when our hearts are afflicted by isolation?

Once again, we find that ancient wisdom and modern science are aligned in their response to loneliness: participate in community to expand relationships (R in PERMA) and draw upon signature strengths.

When Loneliness Strikes: Meet Diane and Marty

In the spring of 2009, Diane and Marty, a couple in their late sixties, moved into a studio apartment next door to my family. As they were trying to fit an enormous amount of furniture and personal items into their very small space, we welcomed them to the building. While Marty unpacked, Diane explained that they were downsizing and relocating from the Upper East Side apartment in New York City where they had lived for over twenty-five years.

A few days later, Diane was sitting in my office at the synagogue. The doorman had told her I was a rabbi, and she needed to talk.

Apparently, she and Marty had known Bernie Madoff[157] for over twenty years. They had almost everything invested with him and had lost it all. Diane had left her teaching job a few years ago, but at the age of sixty-three, she now had no choice but to go back to work.

Marty had retired from his law firm, but he couldn't bring himself to return to his office. The situation had broken him, and he was upset, angry, and depressed. He could barely get out of bed each day. Although they were part of the legal case against Madoff, they did not expect to see a dime. Diane was scared and unsure of what to do.

I sympathized. Diane and Marty were about the same age as my own parents when they retired. I could not imagine what life would be like for them if they had to endure what this family was facing.

We continued talking, and I tested to see if she could begin to imagine a hopeful pathway forward. Diane realized that she had to be the strong one. Marty was a shell of the man she had spent the last forty-five years with. We talked about the trauma they had just endured. It appeared that Marty had turned inward and was feeling isolated. I explained that this was a sign that he needed help and that loneliness can lead to broader health issues. With that, Diane quickly left my office. I did not see her again until four months later she was standing in the lobby of our building.

Diane explained that as a result of the Madoff scandal, Marty had suffered a heart attack. They were now living in a nursing home in Boston, near their daughter. Things were not looking good, so she had come back to get a few things and was quickly heading back to Boston. I have not seen or heard from them since. I've thought of them over the years, especially when I think of how the effects of trauma, financial ruin, job loss, and other life events can lead people, like Marty, to self-isolate.

Loneliness is something that most people will contend with at different times and for different reasons. There is not a single antidote to loneliness, but I am convinced that the virtues and practices we are exploring in this book represent a positive step to reducing loneliness and isolation.

Physical and Emotional Effects of Loneliness on Well-Being

Marty is not unique. There is a large and growing population of people who feel lonely and isolated. Many of us have these feelings every day to a greater or lesser extent, and I've counseled enough people at all stages of life to know that loneliness is a very real condition that exists for everyone, from young children through the elderly.

Ironically, some of the busiest and most decorated professionals I know feel lonely. Although many of us are in constant contact with others through our personal electronics, many still feel lonely, isolated, and empty. Wealth, educational background, beauty, physical prowess, and personal and professional affiliations don't make the difference—even committed couples feel it; loneliness and isolation are an epidemic in our modern world.

We cannot regard feelings of loneliness as purely emotional. Research on loneliness shows that it can have a significant impact on our physical health as part of our overall well-being.[158] People who feel lonely are more likely to inflict harm on their bodies and even take their own lives.[159] They often have higher rates of heart disease and weaker immune systems.[160] One study showed that loneliness is as dangerous to our health as obesity, smoking, and alcoholism.[161] In fact, the subjective feeling of loneliness increases the risk of premature death by 26 percent.[162]

Some may have the impression that the elderly are the most isolated and lonely among all social groups, but studies show otherwise. In 2018, over twenty thousand people were surveyed for loneliness in the United States, and the younger generations (Gen Y and Z) responded with more loneliness than the older generations. While some may imagine the epidemic of loneliness is a result of online gaming and social media, it has more to do with the lack of real social connections and authentic relationships.[163] As the Bible states, "It is not good for people to be alone."

"Ayekah—Where Are You?": The Lonely Path of God

The Torah begins with the story of Creation. God creates the heavens and the earth, and on the sixth day, Adam is created. There is a story that imagines Adam looking at all the pairs of animals, two by two marching along, and giving them names. But as soon as Adam is done naming each animal, he turns to God and says, "Everyone has a partner, but I have none."[164] Adam is alone, and he is lonely. Aware now that he needs a mate to satisfy his loneliness, God immediately creates Eve, and together Adam and Eve live in the Garden of Eden.

Today, people face the same issues of loneliness that our biblical ancestors faced. Like Adam, many single people feel lonely and incomplete until they find a spouse or partner. How many individuals and couples without children feel isolated until they have or adopt children? How many people suffering with illness or disease feel isolated and on the fringe of our faith communities?

A parent in my congregation was having a conflict with her teenage daughter, who wanted to start riding the New York City subways by herself. She knew of the tracking app for phones that enables anyone to know the whereabouts of a person who gives permission to "share location." However, she was not comfortable because her daughter could turn the app off anytime she chose.

Nevertheless, they downloaded the app, and mom was following online. The daughter was riding the subway; however, she was not coming home on time, nor was she responding to mom's repeated text messages of "Where are you? Where are you? Where are you?"

The Torah presents God in a similar way. Early in the Book of Genesis, Adam and Eve exhibit some independence and choose to eat from the Tree of Knowledge. God cries out to them, "*Ayekah*—Where are you?"[165] God can see them in the garden, but God does not feel connected to Adam and Eve. We might imagine that God feels lonely.

There is an ancient story that imagines God and the Jewish people as twin siblings. When one sibling feels something, so does the other. When the people are suffering and lonely, God says, "When [they] call on Me, I will answer [them]. I will be with [them] in distress."[166] It's why God chose the burning bush as the place to speak to Moses, saying, "Do you realize that I live in trouble, just as Israel lives in trouble? From within this thorn bush, I am suffering with them."[167]

This is Judaism's way of expressing that the relationship God has with humanity means that we are not alone. In moments of distress, perhaps especially in lonely moments, we have the eternal promise that the Divine is with us.

Life in Isolation: The Ancient Israelites

What could be more isolating than slavery and the loss of self-determination? The Jewish narrative from slavery to freedom shaped three thousand years of spiritual lessons, which are retold every year during the holiday of Passover. The Passover seder is a reenactment, in story, food, prayer, and song, of God freeing the Israelites from isolation and empowering Moses, Miriam, and Aaron to lead them to freedom.

Ironically, while the Exodus narrative involves elements of slavery and isolation, the observance of the Passover seder itself has tremendous potential to be an antidote to loneliness. The seder is a relationship experience that brings friends and family together to share a meal, and participants have rich opportunities to engage in a night of deep questions and conversation about history, society, and culture.

As the Passover seder concludes, there is the final act. The door is opened for Elijah the Prophet. The spirit of Elijah inspires us to accomplish more good deeds in the year to come and to improve our world so that "next year we'll all be together in Jerusalem"—not necessarily the city in Israel, but a Jerusalem that is our spiritual symbol of well-being and happiness for all humanity.

The famous song "Jerusalem of Gold," by Naomi Shemer, describes the dream of a place where the "shofar calls" us to be. On the surface, we're called to the Old City in Jerusalem, Israel. But on a deeper level, we're called spiritually to "Jerusalem," literally "City of Peace," which represents peace, harmony, and unity. And that Jerusalem is the "Jerusalem" that comes from bringing positivity to the world. Well-being and happiness are not simply practical ideas; they are deeply spiritual concepts.

Religion and the Strength of Spirituality

Many people tell me they are spiritual but not religious, and vice versa, they are religious but not spiritual. How people define these terms is very personal, but their ancient meanings are different from how we generally understand them in a modern context.

The word "religion" comes from the Latin word *religio*, meaning "respect for what is sacred, reverence for the gods, sense of right, moral obligation, sanctity, obligation, the bond between man and the gods."[168] Peter Harrison, author of *The Territories of Science and Religion*, writes that "in the ancient and medieval world, *religio* was understood as an individual virtue . . . never as doctrine, practice, or actual source of knowledge. Religion as we define it today, with over ten thousand types of religions in the world and with over 84% of humanity identifying with a specific religion, is a rather modern invention."[169]

While the word "religion" is never used in the Bible, *religio* points to something that is very important in Judaism: virtues. We have used the ideas of virtues and character strengths interchangeably in this book, because we are interested in improving well-being and happiness in people's lives and in the world through activating people's individual strengths (i.e., virtues).

Positive Judaism views *religio* as a pathway to well-being, and spirituality as one of the many virtues that promote happiness. Spirituality, *ruchni'ut* in Hebrew, is having faith in a higher purpose and expressing connection to and interest in the unknowable and unseen. The medieval Jewish philosopher Bachya ibn Pakuda believed that "there are ten gates our Creator has opened to mankind so that we may enter into the domain of spirituality."

These metaphoric gates represent various principles of a person's spiritual life, starting with acknowledging the unity of God.[170]

Those who have spirituality as one of their signature strengths may feel driven by their deep faith and their search for the sacred. As to whether people consider themselves spiritual and/or religious, the benefits for well-being are the same. As Dr. Sonja Lyubomirsky states, "Religious people are relatively happier than the non-religious, have superior mental health, cope better with stressors, have more satisfying marriages, use drugs and alcohol less often, are physically healthier, and live longer lives."[171]

> **JEWISH HAPPINESS VIRTUE**
> **SPIRITUALITY**
> Spirituality, *ruchni'ut*, is having faith in a higher purpose and expressing connection to and interest in the unknowable and unseen.

JEWISH WELL-BEING PRACTICE
The Passover Seder

The Passover seder is the ultimate Jewish well-being experience that draws on all the elements of PERMA, character strengths, and broaden-and-build (see the strengths-based "Positive Judaism Passover Seder" in appendix C). The seder is an opportunity to gather multiple generations of children and adults, family and friends, and community to share a ceremonial meal together and receive all the benefits of positive emotions, relationships, and meaning as the story is read in the haggadah.

Even though the seder may be an annual affair, the lessons we teach and learn through the seder experience can be applied all year long. The words that begin the Passover seder describe a vision where nobody is lonely or isolated: "Let all who are hungry come and eat; let all who are in need come and join in the celebration of Passover." In the eleventh century, Moses Maimonides taught that the greatest joy of the holiday is not eating and drinking, but inviting people to the seder who may otherwise have been alone.

Yet the seder is more than just an antidote for loneliness; it sets the table for total inclusivity. Adding an orange to the seder plate has become a symbol of inclusivity that recognizes those who have been traditionally marginalized in the Jewish community: women, those differently abled, LGBTQ+, Jews of color, and others.

When every person at the seder table is invited to read part of the story aloud, we are taught that every voice is important. This type of radical inclusion can be a spiritual practice that furthers the positive well-being of every participant. Hearts and minds are positively opened to whatever may appear to be different, which contributes to making the Passover seder the ultimate Jewish well-being experience.

For Personal Reflection

1. What practical actions have you taken to counteract feelings of loneliness?

2. How does your community include people who feel lonely or may be isolated?

3. In what ways are your signature strengths represented in the Passover seder?

11 *"Gam zu l'tovah—*this too is for good."

—Nachum Ish Gamzu, Babylonian Talmud, *Ta'anit* 21a

When the Work Is Not Working: Job Loss and Forced Career Change

Losing a job can be traumatic. One's career, self-esteem, and financial situation can all be thrown into question in a heartbeat. People may find themselves involuntarily out of work as a result of their actions or through no fault of their own, causing massive emotional disruption. For most people, the loss of a job is more than just losing income, it can also bring a change in personal status, daily routine, and feelings of purpose, identity, and self-worth. But perhaps the greatest tragedy is the despair and even suicide that can follow a job or financial crisis—in fact, suicide rates are highest for middle-aged white men following such a crisis.[172]

Ancient stories from Jewish tradition offer us the wisdom to put job loss into a larger context and to see the loss as an opportunity for growth. Often these losses are blessings in disguise. To discover these blessings, modern science recommends keeping a daily gratitude journal and taking time to reconnect with one's best self to emerge from this loss in a healthier and happier place.

"Thank You for Firing Me": Meet Roger

At fifty-six years old, Roger had just lost his third job in as many years when he came to talk to me. He had been working as a financial analyst, and he was recently divorced and financially overextended, with huge rent payments, college tuition costs, and credit card debt.

After he described the details of his firing, I asked Roger how he felt. He shared that he could barely find the strength to get out of bed. His feelings were palpable and normal. Exhaustion and self-isolation are signs of depression, as well as typical reactions to job loss. Suicide rates for individuals like Roger are also high following a job or financial crisis. I was concerned, but nothing he said raised any alarms.

We agreed to meet again the following week, and he showed up late, unshaven, bags under his eyes, unsure as to why he had come. When people say something like, "I'm not sure what I'm doing here," it's a signal to me that they may be feeling that way about their life, as in "I'm not sure what my purpose is anymore." My sense was that the financial industry was not a good match for Roger.

Roger did not discuss his financial pressures, his lack of sleep, or conversations he'd been having with his close friends, children, or family members. Instead, he described in detail what happened to him during each of his three firing experiences. He was stuck on the firing episodes.

I shared a story, a Jewish tale about a scholar named Zusya who was nearing his death. He gathered his students close to him and said, "In the coming world, they will not ask me, 'Why were you not more like Moses, our great leader?' They will ask me, 'Why were you not more like Zusya?'"

I explained that discovering your best self means choosing the life you want to live, not the life somebody else expects for you.

Roger sat there and said nothing. Finally, he said, "My grandfather told me that story when I was a kid. It's all I needed to hear." Then he left.

A year later, I learned that Roger had left my office and done something bold. He had gone on a personal retreat to think about what he really wanted to be doing with his life. Following that, he downsized to a less expensive apartment and got a temporary job teaching elementary school math at an inner-city school.

While this new path was a huge challenge, he was happy teaching and finally felt like he was doing something good with his life. He had found his calling—helping young people—especially the kids in a tough neighborhood. He had just sent a five-word postcard to his old boss that read, "Thank you for firing me."

Every Loss Creates Opportunity

Roger turned a loss into a new life opportunity by drawing on his character strengths. In his life transition, he learned several truths of well-being. It's not about the money, it's about the meaning. It's not about prestige, it's about impact. And it's not about living up to another's expectations for you, it's about finding the life that wants to live in you.

In 2008, when the financial markets collapsed, Ellen came to see me. She had shown up to work to find the doors of her building locked. A sign on the door read, "In an emergency meeting yesterday, this company was sold, including this office building. Your personal belongings will be shipped to the address we have on file. All work has ceased. Please refer to your employment agreement for further information or dial the 800 number below. We apologize for this inconvenience. Thank you."

Ellen had been at that company for nine years. She had just bought a house, and the payments were expensive. She was in a state of panic.

Nevertheless, for the next three months, she got dressed every day as if for the office, left the house on time, took the train to the city, and spent all day looking for jobs. Ellen felt such shame and confusion, she didn't tell her husband about losing her job, but he knew something was wrong. She was irritable, not sleeping well, didn't want to leave the house on the weekends, didn't want to see people socially. She was totally stressed out and lost.

Experts tell us that people in situations similar to Ellen's have an increased risk of feeling shame, anxiety, depression, or stress and are prone to more drug and alcohol use, illness, and physical problems following a job loss.[173] However, depending on how we can activate our character strengths, there can be another way. For example:

1. Bernie Marcus was fired from his job at Handy Dan and then went on to start the successful home improvement company Home Depot. Home Depot employs thousands of workers, serving communities all over North America, and his foundation supports education and social causes all over the world.

2. Author J. K. Rowling, who wrote the *Harry Potter* series of books, was once fired from her job as a secretary. She was a single mother, without a job, living month to month on food stamps, and spent her days at a cafe in Edinburgh, Scotland, writing her first *Harry Potter* novel. Today, she is the most financially successful woman in the United Kingdom, and millions of people, young and old, have been entertained by her books and the movies based on them.

3. Comedian Jerry Seinfeld got removed from one of his first paid roles on the television show *Benson* after a few episodes, with no warning. He showed up to rehearsal and realized he had been written out of the script. He went back to stand-up comedy, and soon a talent scout for the *Tonight Show* was in the audience and booked him. From there, his career took off.

4. Home-life expert Martha Stewart got fired from her job as a stockbroker on Wall Street in 1973 and decided to start a local catering business. She published her first cookbook ten years later and went on have a significant influence in homes and kitchens across the world.

What allowed these people to thrive in the face of job loss? They are not superhuman. They are like anyone seeking to flourish and thrive in their lives. They were able to activate their character strengths of resilience, optimism, creativity, and perseverance to guide them through the rough patches. The point is not that these folks became financially successful; the point is that with hard work, personal clarity, and the right timing, they found a way to lift themselves up and to find the life that wanted to live in them.

Staying Positive with Gratitude

A recent study on emotional recovery after job loss determined that people who had lost their jobs found new and better work significantly faster if they wrote about their experience for thirty minutes each day. The study discovered that journaling helped these individuals reduce intense emotions and change perspective on negative feelings, thoughts, and reactions.[174]

These are similar results to what research tells us about people who keep a gratitude journal, writing down three to five things for which they are grateful every day.[175] Focusing on the positive fills the mind with good thoughts. Studies show that activating feelings of gratitude has the capacity to increase natural, feel-good chemicals such as dopamine, serotonin, and oxytocin. All this stimulates the brain, resulting in greater emotional and physical well-being, which is expressly needed after a job loss.

Expressing gratitude is a central pillar of positive Jewish living. The idea is that no matter what is happening in life, there is always a reason to be grateful. On being grateful, the wise Rabbi Mordechai Yosef Leiner, the Radziner Rebbe, taught, "One who crosses the sea and survives a storm thanks God. Why not thank God when there is no storm? One who survives an illness thanks God. Why not one who escapes altogether?"

Gratitude is one of the most important virtues and happiness practices because it generates positive emotions. *Hakarat hatov*, literally "recognizing the good," is the Hebrew phrase for gratitude, the ability to

> **JEWISH HAPPINESS VIRTUE**
> **GRATITUDE**
> Gratitude, *hakarat hatov*, is the ability to be thankful, to be aware of the good, and to take time to express appreciation.

be thankful, to be aware of the good, and to take time to express appreciation. Those who lack gratitude for the good in their lives often exude an air of entitlement. In the words of Rabbi Nachman of Breslov, "Gratitude rejoices with her sister joy and is always ready to light a candle and have a party. Gratitude doesn't much like the old cronies of boredom, despair, and taking life for granted."

The Talmud recounts the tale of Nachum Ish Gamzu, who was destitute, blind, and without the use of his limbs. And yet, no matter what happened to him, his response was always, "*Gam zu l'tovah*—this too is for good."[176]

The daily morning prayer called Modeh Ani, meaning "I give thanks," captures the essence of gratitude: "I offer gratitude before You, living and eternal One, for You have mercifully restored my soul within me." This reminds us that every day is a new day, and no matter what is going on, we are alive, and that is the greatest gift and a true fortune.

Yet, according to one of the oldest sources of homiletic midrash, gratitude will be everlasting in the next world, where "all sacrifices will cease, except for the thanksgiving offering, which will never cease. All prayers too will cease, except for the prayer of gratitude, which will never cease." Here we learn that the sages believed that even in a heavenly world in which religion will be obsolete, gratitude will remain steadfast, a pillar of existence.[177]

"Just Get Going"

The ancient Israelites certainly had worries, stresses, and fears. They started as slaves and then walked endlessly through the desert. At one point, the entire community was frustrated, exhausted, and empty. They said to Moses, "Let's turn back to Egypt." But with great leadership and inspiration, Moses said to the people, "Have no fear! Stand by, and witness the deliverance which [God] will work for you today . . . hold your peace!" Then God said to Moses, "Why do you cry out to Me? Tell the Israelites to [just get going]."[178]

"Just get going" became an important mantra for me in 2010 when I experienced a surprise job change. I was thirty-seven years old, with two young children at home, and when the term of my employment contract came to an end, the board of directors decided that it was time for them to go in a different direction with their professional leadership. This was the first time in my life that a job had ended for me involuntarily. I was off-balance and in new territory.

Though I had counseled others through this very situation, I had never experienced the loss of a job myself. I was anxious, confused, and stressed. There were things that I loved about that job, but truth be told, it was not the right fit for me personally or professionally. I was the executive director for a young Jewish organization whose mission I believed in deeply, but I was not doing the work that lived in me. I wanted to be a rabbi, a pastor, a teacher. They needed a CEO to do the important tasks of a chief adminis-trator—management, board development, financial accountability, strategic planning, and so on—all essential to the health of any company, just not my area of expertise or passion. After six years of doing the wrong job, I needed to relearn what was most important to me.

It was a real growth period for me, and one afternoon a close friend asked if I had thought about starting a synagogue. She knew I loved being a rabbi, and the fast-growing neighborhood where we lived needed a new Jewish center. My heart was deeply committed to serving the Jewish com-munity, and as she spoke words of deep support, my inner voice was saying, "Just get going."

Six months later, and with the help of many friends and colleagues, we invited everyone we knew for the first Shabbat gathering of Tamid: The Downtown Synagogue. About forty-five people showed up. The first step of the journey was complete. The home of what would become a commu-nity of Positive Judaism was born.

A Mystical Understanding of Your Best Self

Jewish mysticism believes that the purpose of our lives is to be our best selves in order to contribute to the union and perfection of the universe. As we learned in chapter 3, our purpose is to capture the fragments of light that scattered into the universe during Creation and reunite them into a harmonious wholeness by living our best life possible.

The Jewish concept of *tikun* is the mystical notion of righting a world that is out of balance. *Tikun olam*, "repairing the world," is the call to make the world a better place and to perform good deeds from a place of loving-kindness. There are endless areas in need of *tikun* all over the world. The same is true for every individual. When we are not living in harmony with our true self, we are out of cosmic alignment. It is by bringing our best selves to the world that we contribute positively to the harmony of the universe.

This is a critical message for every working person who goes through a job transition. A job loss creates a flexion point, a natural break, a pause in a person's life. One can choose to bounce right over to the next job, but with the right support and patience, this moment can become an opportunity for real personal growth, a *tikun atzmi* (repair of self), a chance to take a minute to explore the state of your current self. A job loss can be a gift because the person you were when you took the job you lost has evolved and grown. The new you may benefit from some time to consider a new work direction.

We've already discussed the research that shows there is only a slight relationship between wealth, income, and happiness. Therefore, if wealth is not the driver for happiness, perhaps it is time to find the job, the work, and the career direction that will align your deepest personal purpose with how you are spending most of your time every day.

When I ask adults to tell me about themselves, most will tell me what they do professionally, their job title, and where they work. Sometimes they even tell me what they do before they tell me their name. "I'm the vice president for external affairs at the largest convener of foreign and global sales. Hi, I'm Mark, nice to meet you."

Interestingly however, when I ask young people to tell me about themselves, they describe their personal interests and hobbies. "I love to play soccer, and my team won on Saturday." "I'm a dancer, and I like to do art and read." For adults, this might sound something like this: "My name is Joan. I am living my dream as a book editor, helping writers find their voice and share their ideas in words." Aligning a person's work with their natural strengths and unique purpose is one of the key answers to a person's well-being. We only live once, so make your purpose your work and your life.

Viktor Frankl wrote, "The meaning of life is to help others to find the meaning of theirs."[179] Some people love the outdoors and want to be outdoors all the time, but they have a desk job they loathe. Could there be a job in the outdoors that would be perfect for them? Some people love the arts but think there is no money in design, fashion, music, theater, or writing poetry, and so they suffer quietly in jobs they dislike. That's a waste of time and a waste of a life.

We learn a lot about a person's real life at funerals through the eulogies that are shared. Most speak about the devotion the person had to their family. Many reflect on a specific hobby, pastime, or vacation spot that brought the deceased immense joy and great satisfaction.

And finally, said in any number of different ways, are the regrets. "At the end of Dad's life, he shared with me that he wished he had worked less and spent more time playing with his kids and grandkids." Or, "She was a devoted surgeon, but she really loved sailing and being on the water; that gave her the greatest happiness." Or in the case of a young person, "He loved the stage, but there was no money in theater, so he got into financial services, which he never liked. I just wish he had done what he wanted with this life; you never know when it's going to be over."

We should not be scared into living our passions out of a sense of panic that time is short and life is fleeting. Rather, in the words of Rabbi Menachem Mendel Schneerson, "If you see what needs to be repaired and how to repair it, then you have found a piece of the world that God has left for you to complete. But if you see what needs to be done, and you choose not to act on it, it is you who needs repair."[180]

Express Gratitude by Volunteering

Volunteering and helping others can make us happier by giving us a "helper's high."[181] It helps focus the mind on doing good, which can affect our sense of self-worth, strengthen our abilities, and reinforce the feeling that we are making a positive difference in the world.

Giving back is especially important during times when we feel sad and disconnected, because it offers a boost in positivity and a sense of gratitude, optimism, and compassion. Author Leon Uris said, "The only thing that is going to save mankind is if enough people live their lives for something or someone other than themselves."[182]

There is a long history in Judaism of helping others in need, dating back to the biblical era when farmers were commanded to leave the produce on the corners of their field untouched for the poor to come and gather willingly.[183] Feeding the poor has always been a mitzvah, a commanded good deed, in Jewish life. There are unlimited opportunities to volunteer and give back—to perform your act of *tikun olam*, to make the world a better place—and simultaneously bring you closer to a sense of gratitude for what you have and who you are.

For Personal Reflection

1. What motivates your sense of *tikun*, repair?

2. What areas of need inspire you to want to make a difference in the world?

3. What service organization or nonprofit would you like to support with your time and effort?

12 "Even in darkness it is possible to create light."
—ELIE WIESEL

Upside Down: Dealing with Financial Trouble

As money is one of the five areas of well-being, when financial problems arise, a person's overall well-being and happiness can suffer greatly. Job loss, unexpected medical costs, loans, credit card debt, divorce, addiction, and other sources of financial problems are stressful and can lead to health problems, relationship challenges, and strained connections to friends and community. Money problems are real and taxing, yet, "even in darkness it is possible to create light," taught Elie Wiesel.[184]

To create light in a time of darkness takes concerted effort, a willingness to genuinely take responsibility for one's situation, and to focus on improving total well-being (health, relationships, work, community, and finances). When we take responsibility for our life and happiness, the lessons learned during a financial crisis, large or small, can ultimately lead to even higher levels of well-being, as we will explore in this chapter.

"The Bankruptcy Was God's Plan": Meet Steve

A man I had never met came to the synagogue offices asking to see me. He was well-dressed, in his late thirties, and had walked in saying he urgently needed to speak privately with a rabbi.

"My name is Steve and I run a business in the office building next door." Albeit calm and focused, he said there was a lot of chaos over there. I ushered him into my office, where he immediately began to tell me that his company filed for bankruptcy last week.

"It's not great but, *baruch Hashem* [praise God], I've gotten through it before and with God's blessing, I will again. I don't need to tell you, when God wants something to happen, it happens!

"I've always been close with my rabbis, because they are close to God," explained Steve. "Whenever I had problems, I always spoke to rabbis. They helped remind me that everything is God's plan. My first company also filed for bankruptcy, but it was God's plan."

After listening to all of this, it was clear to me that Steve needed to take more responsibility for his own life and the decisions he made. I expressed that while God may have a plan for his life, I was curious to know how he makes sense of God's plan today. I imagined that his employees know about the bankruptcy, and they will need to find new jobs. Steve had responsibility for the financial well-being of a lot of people—employees, investors, creditors, and himself—which must certainly put a lot of pressure on him.

Bluntly, I asked if he thought his employees and investors thought this was according to God's plan. Why would God plan that he face a second bankruptcy and now have a reputation as a businessman who leads companies to failure? I was curious to know if he could respond to why God would want all this trouble for all these people, including him.

While he took that in, I went on to remind him of the Jewish idea of *cheshbon hanefesh*, an accounting of the soul, and the idea that we all must think about and care for others. Pensively, Steve told me he doesn't know why God made it this way, but God did. Not willing to give up on Steve, I recalled Elie Wiesel's wisdom that light can come from darkness.

I encouraged Steve to close his eyes and pray, like the men and women at the Western Wall in Jerusalem who write their prayers on notes and place them in the cracks of the stones. I did not want him to tell me the words, because I sensed that there was something very personal he wanted to say to God.

He closed his eyes, quietly moved his lips, stood up quickly, and said,

"Amen." I could tell he was ready to leave. I shook his hand and wished him well.

I've learned that how a person imagines the role that God plays in their lives is very personal and very individual. In reaction to Steve's worldview, I believe that God does not intervene in our lives to absolve us of responsibility, rather God holds us responsible for our actions. In this respect, God is the source of our strengths to overcome challenges, not our escape clause.

One could rightly claim that despite his challenges, Steve's view that all is according to God's plan may be an effective coping mechanism. However, to pass the Positive Judaism test, our beliefs, attitudes, and actions must increase happiness and positivity not only for ourselves but for others as well. Perhaps his staff and his investors went forward to better lives after they left Steve—I'll never know. To me, the primary concern was Steve's mind-set on the day we met and my belief that to increase well-being, people need to take responsibility and accountability for their actions. Ultimately, this is the way to happiness and well-being.

Taking 100 Percent Responsibility for Everything in Your Life

While the practical consequences of money trouble—like not being able to pay bills, downsizing, taking loans, or filing for personal bankruptcy—are complex, the mental and emotional burden can be overwhelming as well. Family, friends, and even children are all at risk for stress and anxiety. Financial strain can be the result of many factors, including divorce, illness, or job loss, and can result in self-isolation. On some level, each of these issues can be the source, result, or part of the individual problem, because everything is connected, and everything influences our well-being.

Personal bankruptcy presents its own unique challenges, for when someone sinks deeply into debt, they often take others along for the ride. Most people do everything possible before reaching that final legal step of declaring bankruptcy, including borrowing money from friends and family to try to recover. Unfortunately, these people are frequently left holding the bag.

So, while the debt might be legally lifted, new problems may emerge, like dealing with feelings of regret, guilt, and shame. This is where the growth opportunity exists. As a Jewish proverb teaches, "He who cannot endure the bad will not live to see the good."

I have witnessed the emotional cost of bankruptcy on the lives of individuals and families, and it can be devastating. Some people blame or pass their responsibility to others or, as in Steve's case, believe this was God's plan. If they can accept that the factors that led them into bankruptcy were partly under their influence and included some combination of bad luck and bad judgment, there is much to be gained. There can be important lessons learned about perseverance, self-actualization, and personal independence.

The Yiddish poet and author Sholom Aleichem taught, "No matter how bad things get, you've got to go on living." This suggests that regardless of our challenges, our stresses, and our difficulties, we must find a way to persevere. Some people have a hard time persevering on their own or accepting responsibility for their actions, because it is so much easier to place the blame on others. However, when we take responsibility for and face up to life's challenges, we become equally ready to take responsibility for our well-being and happiness.

Perseverance, *hatmada* in Hebrew, is the ability to be industrious, to complete the task, and to persist in the face of obstacles. The fifteenth-century Spanish rabbi Isaac ben Moses Arama wrote, "Personal effort and perseverance contribute in major part to eventual success. In fact, any negligence or laziness is rated as sinful when circumstances seem to have called for exertion of the self."[185]

> **JEWISH HAPPINESS VIRTUE**
> **PERSEVERANCE**
> Perseverance, *hatmada*, is the ability to be industrious, to complete the task, and to persist in the face of obstacles.

Perseverance is an important character strength that allows us to continue in the face of opposition. Especially during a time of financial pressure, drawing on signature strengths and growing in perseverance allows us to learn from mistakes and grow toward taking responsibility for everything in our lives. This is like taking a true *cheshbon hanefesh*, an accounting of the soul.

Cheshbon Hanefesh: Accounting of the Soul

Cheshbon hanefesh, an accounting of the soul, is a spiritual stocktaking of one's inner life. It's a step-by-step journey of introspection and self-understanding to expose weaknesses and help us become humbler and more self-aware. This is an important process for anyone enduring a life transition and can help reset your life after a divorce, accident, illness, job loss, financial failure, or other challenges.

In 1812, Rabbi Mendel Satanover authored a book called *Cheshbon Hanefesh* (accounting of the soul). He described a process of self-growth that draws upon thirteen virtues and a daily practice to meditate upon them. Some write each virtue on a card and refer to them all throughout the day. Others keep a journal and write daily about each virtue in a free-form flow of consciousness. One traditional approach is to spend an entire week focused on one of the thirteen virtues and to repeat this cycle four times during the year, for a total of fifty-two weeks. This traditional method has seen a renaissance with the contemporary Mussar movement led by Rabbi Ira Stone and Alan Morinis.

To engage in an accounting of the soul is to contemplate ideas and virtues using a methodical process toward personal transformation. You may choose to reflect on the ten virtues outlined in this book, reflect on a selection of the twenty-four character strengths, or consider another list that suits you. Whatever the approach, taking an accounting of the soul is meant to bring to the conscious mind that which is unconscious. Meditation is a good technique to gain a better understanding of how our mind works and to make it an ally in our thoughts and actions. Having control of the mind is part of the process of taking responsibility for our lives and influencing our well-being and happiness.

Mindfulness and Meditation

Practicing meditation is a proven tool in becoming mindful. Meditation master Sharon Salzberg teaches that "all beings want to be happy, yet so very few know how. It is out of ignorance that any of us cause suffering, for ourselves or for others."[186]

There has been much interest in the effects that mindfulness meditation has on our physical and mental health. The United States National Institutes of Health reports that a regular mindfulness practice has five significant positive influences on our lives:[187]

1. Reduces stress and anxiety

2. Reduces and may treat depression

3. Increases physical health and boosts immune systems

4. Improves mental cognition and reduces distractions

5. Boosts happiness and well-being

One of the more interesting findings to emerge from mindfulness meditation research is the impact on the neuroplasticity of the brain, the brain's ability to rewire and restructure itself. Author and mindfulness teacher Dr. Ryan Niemiec writes, "Lab studies on meditators have shown that repetitive mindfulness practice derives positive changes in plasticity leading to greater emotional balance, compassion, happiness, and the buffering of stress and trauma which reflect greater mental and physical well-being."[188]

Mindfulness meditation has a long tradition in Judaism. Following the Amidah, the centerpiece of the daily Jewish prayer service, there is time for personal and quiet meditation. The eleventh-century Jewish philosopher Bachya ibn Pakuda taught that "words are the shell, meditation is the kernel. Words are the body of the prayer, and meditation is the spirit."[189]

JEWISH WELL-BEING PRACTICE
Meditation

The Hebrew word for meditation is *hitbodedut*, "to be with oneself." For people serious about making positive change, mindfulness meditation is a proven path for increasing happiness. It can strengthen your ability to cope with financial trouble or any other stresses that life throws your way. It can create inner space to develop character strengths like perseverance, resilience, and optimism, just to name a few. To begin or to expand your current practice, there are apps, books, online audio resources, and mindfulness centers that host meditation classes and workshops.

There are many ways to meditate, but a common practice is to find a place to sit quietly and comfortably so that you can be in the present without distraction. Some elect to practice breathing exercises to calm the mind and the nervous system and to follow the pattern of thought that crosses the mind like a flowing river. Be patient. Be open. Be nonjudgmental.

These are some verses that may be useful to repeat and reflect upon during meditation:[190]

- In recognition of divine healing:
  Baruch Atah Adonai, Eloheinu Melech ha'olam, Rofei cholim.
  Praised be the Eternal our God, Healer of the sick.[191]

- In recognition of anxiety and worry:
  Yismach Moshe b'marnat chelko.
  Moses was satisfied with his portion.[192]

- In recognition of fear and distress:
  B'yado afkid ruchi, b'eit ishan, v'a'irah, v'im ruchi g'viyati, Adonai li v'lo ira.
  Into God's hands I entrust my spirit, when I sleep and when I wake; and with my spirit and my body also, God is with me, I will not fear.[193]

- In recognition of insecurity and vulnerability:
  Adonai karov l'chol korav, l'chol asher yikra'uhu ve'emet.
  God is near to all who cry out, to all who cry out to God in truth.[194]

- In honor of gratitude and appreciation:
  Zeh hayom asah Adonai, nagilah v'nism'cha vo.
  This is the day that God has made; let us rejoice and be glad in it.[195]

For Personal Reflection

1. During financial difficulty and stress, what strategies or practices have been helpful to your maintaining well-being?

2. In what ways could taking 100 percent responsibility for your life improve your overall well-being?

3. How could meditation have a positive impact on your ability to cope with a financial crisis or any other stress in your life?

Part Four

The Journey Forward: The Future of Positive Judaism

At the end of the Torah, Moses stands upon Mount Nebo and reflects on his life as he looks forward into the Promised Land. His journey is nearing the end, but he sees a prosperous future that will flow with milk and honey for the people of Israel. This farewell message in the Torah imagines hope and optimism, not an ending but rather the start of a new era.

The same is true for us. We each have the potential for the start of a new era of our own. My hope is that the messages of Positive Judaism inspire you to put authentic happiness and well-being at the center of your life, in your family, and within your community.

Let us reflect on this Jewish journey to well-being and happiness. We've learned that well-being and happiness come from increasing positive emotions, deepening engagement in everything we do, strengthening our relationships, enhancing meaning in our life choices, and encouraging one and all to strive for accomplishments. This is the PERMA framework.

We have learned about the twenty-four character strengths and how our signature strengths impact well-being and happiness.

We've examined the five areas of life and explored Jewish wisdom to shine a spotlight on how well-being is affected by the quality of our relationships, our health, our community, our work, and our money.

We have explored the broaden-and-build theory, showing that

increased positive emotions support the upward growth of a person's overall well-being.

Keeping all this in balance is our life's task. There are going to be times when relationships will be strained. There will be times when we are ill and suffering. Loneliness and isolation may creep up on us. We may find ourselves out of work and looking for a new job. And there will inevitably be financial pressures as the global world economy continues to evolve.

But now we have a plan—a plan that pairs three thousand years of ancient wisdom and modern science. We have explored the ten Jewish happiness virtues and can use the ten Jewish well-being practices to guide us and to brace us against life's challenges. Of course, everyone's journey is unique, but now we know how to structure a life of happiness and well-being.

Yet this is just the starting point. Remember the words of Rabbi Israel Salanter: "First a person should put his own house together, then his town, and then the world. In other words, first his own well-being, then his community's well-being, and then the well-being of the world."

Now it is time to activate positivity, happiness, and well-being in our lives, teach it to our children, share it with our family and friends, and give it to the world. As Hillel asked in the first century BCE, "If not now, when?"

A Letter to Readers and Friends

Adopting Positive Judaism in Your Life

Dear readers and friends,

Thank you for reading this book. The people that I have described within come from real-life stories that I've witnessed. Aside from my family members, I protected the identities of all these people by changing their names, ages, and even genders at times. Sometimes the episodes are composite stories that have blended together in my mind over the years. I respect and admire everyone who has shared their truths and intimacies with me, and I would never risk revealing their identities. Of my own life and my family, every story is real, and I want you to know why I chose to share so openly.

There is a tale about a Jewish scholar who lived two thousand years ago. Reb Mordechai loved to teach, and he was beloved by his students. Each day he would explain the teachings of the ancient sages, one by one. He brought to life the biblical stories, by making each lesson relevant to the real lives of his students. This way, the rabbi knew he was preparing them to live in the real world.

One Friday, Reb Mordechai's most inquisitive student did not return to class after lunch. He had snuck into the rabbi's home and climbed under the rabbi's bed.

That Shabbat eve, the rabbi and his wife shared in the most spirited lovemaking. Minutes after, they felt something move beneath their bed. To their great surprise, the rabbi's student appeared.

"What are you doing here?" cried the rabbi.

The student replied, "Reb Mordechai, you always teach that you will prepare us to live in the real world. I am here to learn."

As you've read, I shared my own life experiences to model how I approach the journey of life as a son, a husband, a father, a rabbi, and a citizen of the world. I find strength in the story of Reb Mordechai and his student, and I take to heart that my role as a rabbi is to prepare people to live in the real world.

But for me, it goes one step further. The difference between Reb Mordechai and myself is that I want to do more than just prepare you for life. My hope is to train you to thrive and flourish in your own life by adopting Jewish virtues and practices that have been shown by modern science to raise levels of happiness, well-being, positivity, and life satisfaction.

Now it's up to you to choose to adopt these and other virtues and practices in order to live your best life, achieve authentic happiness, find true love, take responsibility for your actions, find your calling, live every day with purpose, and lastly, have the most positive impact on yourself, your family, and the world around you.

Let us call to mind a beautiful prayer from the Torah. "You shall take to heart the words with which I charge you on this day. You shall teach them to your children. You should recite them when you are at home and when you are away, when you lie down and when you rise up."[196]

My hope for you, your children, and the world is that the words you teach and the words you recite are words of positivity, happiness, and well-being.

Shalom, friend. Here is to well-being in your life and in the lives of the ones you love.

Rabbi Darren Levine

A Letter to Colleagues

Adopting Positive Judaism in Your Community

Dear rabbis, cantors, educators, and Jewish communal professionals,

Positive Judaism is not a new movement or new institution. Positive Judaism is a platform that can be adopted and personalized by you for the individuals, families, communities, and organizations you serve. I'm confident that you will be successful if you keep their happiness and well-being at the top of your agenda.

The three theories of well-being I have focused upon in this book have been proved to raise the level of authentic happiness in the lives of individuals and communities. Focusing on PERMA (positive emotions, engagement, relationships, meaning, and accomplishment), character strengths, and the broaden-and-build concept will teach people how to live their best lives in the five areas of life (relationships, health, community, money, and work). This will increase well-being for all those you influence and will make Judaism relevant and compelling in the twenty-first century.

I believe there have been three key drivers for engagement in Jewish life in the last century: (1) Holocaust memory and anti-Semitism; (2) support for the State of Israel; and (3) the perceived threat of intermarriage (which I do not believe is actually a threat to Jewish continuity). These three motivators still have value. It is important to know history so that we will not repeat mistakes of the past. It is important that the State of Israel exists as a safe haven for Jews. It is important that we positively support all families who want to be part of the Jewish people, warmly welcoming spouses and anyone who wishes to live a Jewish life.

While all of this is a given, my experience has been that most Generation Y Millennials and Generation Z Centennials are far less motivated by these ideas than their parents or grandparents are. None of these ideas are compelling *enough* in the twenty-first century to inspire lifelong Jewish engagement, because the issues and challenges we and our communities face today are quite new and different.

Today, people are looking for a deeper meaning to their lives. They want to live a positive life. They want to live well, enjoy life, thrive, and flourish. Helping people address, consider, and toil with these questions in their lives is what makes religion valuable and compelling. Positive Judaism answers the question "Why be Jewish?" It's not the only answer, but it's very persuasive, because it deals with optimal living, well-being, and happiness.

When Positive Judaism becomes the communal framework, I believe the result will be increased positive emotion, increased civic engagement, improved relationships, and accelerated human advancement among individuals and families. People and communities will be on a path toward greater resilience, optimism, and diversity. They will be able to learn new lessons from hardship, experience work as a calling, act and think with purpose, strengthen their relationships, and act generously. I believe this is our greatest opportunity: to bring positivity, happiness, and well-being to humanity and to the world. This is our journey forward.

In the sacred words of the Book of Proverbs, never forget the value of positivity and happiness in your life, "for they will bestow on you length of days, years of life and well-being."[197]

Todah uv'rachah, thank you for your service to the Jewish people. May you continue to impact the lives of your students and communities with positivity, happiness, and well-being.

Rabbi Darren Levine

A Letter to Religious Leaders of All Faiths

Adopting Positive Religion for the Well-Being of Humanity

Dear religious leaders and clergy of all faiths,

Thank you for having a vision of innovative, expansive, and dynamic religious living. Many of us are committed to motivating our communities and our people to achieve great things. Hopefully your people feel loved, supported, and connected to each other and to God. Now is the time for something new: Positive Religion.

We are globally connected in the twenty-first century, and we will rise or fall like ships in the ocean, together. Rabbi Abraham Joshua Heschel taught, "No religion is an island. We are all connected to each another." This means that well-being, life satisfaction, and happiness for all humankind, regardless of nation, race, or politics, are all interrelated. If we speak to the issues of raising well-being, we will move humanity and our planet forward in a positive direction.

I want to propose a new Pastor's Creed for the twenty-first century: The purpose of religious and spiritual leadership shall be to raise the well-being and happiness of the individuals and communities we serve.

We shall do this by applying some, if not all, of the methods described in this book. My contribution is Positive Judaism, and I'm praying for Positive Christianity, Positive Islam, Positive Buddhism, and the like to emerge in the twenty-first century. The Dalai Lama has already promoted individual happiness as a central pillar in Buddhism. Now it is time to focus on happiness, positivity, and well-being on a global religious scale.

To accomplish this, I envision a White Paper on Positive Religion that will include all aspects of well-being that we have addressed in this book and more. This platform would be rooted in the science of well-being and human advancement and would be a collaborative effort among the global religious community.

On September 25, 2015, I sat among the largest interreligious gathering of faith leaders in the modern era. We came together at the 9/11 Memorial Museum in New York City during Pope Francis's visit. More than three hundred representatives from over a dozen faith communities shared in the program "A Witness to Peace: A Multi-Religious Gathering with Pope Francis." Not only did the pope speak, but prayers and meditations were offered by Muslim, Christian, Buddhist, Hindu, Sikh, and Jewish leaders. This moment showcased the potential that global faith communities can have when we come together for a common cause.

While we need to continue to honor the past and be witness to history, we should also be motivated to envision a future that is witness to increased happiness and well-being. For what could be more important than happiness and well-being guiding the way to human and social advancement on a global scale?

This is the journey forward. I look forward to linking hands with you and bridging our religious islands together in a new way: through positivity, happiness, and well-being.

May peace be upon you and your people, and may we work together to raise the well-being and happiness of humanity in our time.

Rabbi Darren Levine

Appendixes

Appendix A:

Adapted PERMA Well-Being Profiler[198]

Instructions: This profiler will offer an insight into your level of well-being today based on the five elements of PERMA (positive emotion, engagement, relationships, meaning, accomplishment). Think about how you felt in the situations described below during the past month and score them from low (0) to high (10).

Question to consider	Circle low to high (0–10)
P1 In general, how often do you feel anxious?	0 1 2 3 4 5 6 7 8 9 10
E1 How often do you become absorbed in what you are doing?	0 1 2 3 4 5 6 7 8 9 10
R1 To what extent do you receive help and support from others when you feel you need it?	0 1 2 3 4 5 6 7 8 9 10
M1 In general, to what extent do you lead a purposeful and meaningful life?	0 1 2 3 4 5 6 7 8 9 10
A1 How much of the time do you feel you are making progress toward accomplishing your goals?	0 1 2 3 4 5 6 7 8 9 10
P2 In general, how often do you feel positive?	0 1 2 3 4 5 6 7 8 9 10
E2 In general, to what extent do you feel that what you do in your life is valuable and worthwhile?	0 1 2 3 4 5 6 7 8 9 10
R2 To what extent do you feel loved?	0 1 2 3 4 5 6 7 8 9 10
M2 In general, to what extent do you feel that what you do in your life is meaningful and purposeful?	0 1 2 3 4 5 6 7 8 9 10

A2 How often do you achieve the important goals you have set for yourself?	0 1 2 3 4 5 6 7 8 9 10
P3 In general, to what extent do you feel content?	0 1 2 3 4 5 6 7 8 9 10
E3 How often do you lose track of time while doing something you enjoy?	0 1 2 3 4 5 6 7 8 9 10
R3 How satisfied are you with your personal relationships?	0 1 2 3 4 5 6 7 8 9 10
M3 To what extent do you generally feel you have a sense of direction in your life?	0 1 2 3 4 5 6 7 8 9 10
A3 How often are you able to handle your responsibilities?	0 1 2 3 4 5 6 7 8 9 10

Scoring

Add the numbers for each of the categories of questions and divide by 3 to get the average.

P1 + P2 + P3 = _____	*Divide this number by 3 to get your average P score.*	P = _____
E1 + E2 + E3 = _____	*Divide this number by 3 to get your average E score.*	E = _____
R1 + R2 + R3 = _____	*Divide this number by 3 to get your average R score.*	R = _____
M1 + M2 + M3 = _____	*Divide this number by 3 to get your average M score.*	M = _____
A1 + A2 + A3 = _____	*Divide this number by 3 to get your average A score.*	A = _____

Bar Graph Illustration and Definitions

Take your average score results for each of the five PERMA questions and mark them on the bar graph below. This will provide a general view of your PERMA Profile today.

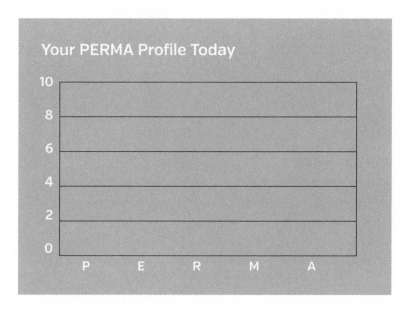

Here is a sample bar graph:

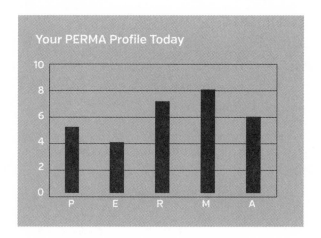

P = Positive Emotions

Emotions are an important part of our well-being. Emotions can range from very negative to very positive and range from high arousal (excitement, explosive) to low arousal (calm, relaxed, sad).

E = Engagement

Engagement refers to being absorbed, interested, and involved in an activity or the world itself. Very high levels of engagement in a particular task is known as the "flow state," in which you are absorbed in your activity and lose all sense of time.

R = Relationships

Relationships refer to feeling loved, supported, and valued by others. Having positive relationships with others is an important part of feeling life is good and going well.

M = Meaning

Meaning refers to having a sense of purpose in life, a direction where life is going, feeling that life is valuable and worth living, or connecting to something larger than ourselves, such as a religious faith, a charity, or a personally meaningful goal.

A = Accomplishment

Accomplishment can be marked not only by honors and awards received, but also by feelings of mastery and achievement. Accomplishment involves staying on top of daily responsibilities, working toward goals, and feeling able to complete tasks large and small.

Measure Overview: Dr. Martin Seligman defines the five pillars of well-being with PERMA in his book *Flourish* (2011). To learn more about PERMA and these results, visit www.authentichappiness.org.

Appendix B:

Signature Strengths Survey©

Step 1

Read the following descriptions of the twenty-four character strengths. Everyone uses these strengths at times. Put a check next to those strengths that are absolutely essential to you, that define who you are as a person, that are part of who you are.

For example, someone who has devoted his life to helping others might choose kindness as one of his essential strengths; someone who prides herself on being able to figure out other people might consider social intelligence key to who she is; and someone who is constantly seeking out new information might consider love of learning to be essential. Most people check just a few essential strengths. Please describe the person you are, not the person you wish you could be. Also, think about your life in general, not how you've behaved in only one or two situations.

Essential Strength	Character Strengths
○	**1. Creativity:** You are viewed as a creative person; you see, do, and/or create things that are of use; you think of unique ways to solve problems and be productive.
○	**2. Curiosity:** You are an explorer; you seek novelty; you are interested in new activities, ideas, and people; you are open to new experiences.
○	**3. Judgment/Critical Thinking:** You are analytical; you examine things from all sides; you do not jump to conclusions, but instead attempt to weigh all the evidence when making decisions.
○	**4. Love of Learning:** You often find ways to deepen your knowledge and experiences; you regularly look for new opportunities to learn; you are passionate about building knowledge.

Essential Strength	Character Strengths
◯	**5. Perspective:** You take the "big picture" view of things; others turn to you for wise advice; you help others make sense of the world; you learn from your mistakes.
◯	**6. Bravery:** You face your fears and overcome challenges and adversity; you stand up for what is right; you do not shrink in the face of pain or inner tension or turmoil.
◯	**7. Perseverance:** You keep going and going when you have a goal in mind; you attempt to overcome all obstacles; you finish what you start.
◯	**8. Honesty:** You are a person of high integrity and authenticity; you tell the truth, even when it hurts; you present yourself to others in a sincere way; you take responsibility for your actions.
◯	**9. Zest:** You are enthusiastic toward life; you are highly energetic and activated; you use your energy to the fullest degree.
◯	**10. Love:** You are warm and genuine to others; you not only share but are open to receiving love from others; you value growing close and intimate with others.
◯	**11. Kindness:** You do good things for people; you help and care for others; you are generous and giving; you are compassionate.
◯	**12. Social Intelligence:** You pay close attention to social nuances and the emotions of others; you have good insight into what makes people "tick"; you seem to know what to say and do in any social situation.
◯	**13. Teamwork:** You are a collaborative and participative member on groups and teams; you are loyal to your group; you feel a strong sense of duty to your group; you always do your share.
◯	**14. Fairness:** You believe strongly in an equal and just opportunity for all; you don't let personal feelings bias your decisions about others; you treat people the way you want to be treated.
◯	**15. Leadership:** You positively influence those you lead; you prefer to lead than to follow; you are very good at organizing and taking charge for the collective benefit of the group.

Essential Strength	Character Strengths
○	**16. Forgiveness:** You readily let go of hurt after you are wronged; you give people a second chance; you are not vengeful or resentful; you accept people's shortcomings.
○	**17. Humility:** You let your accomplishments speak for themselves; you see your own goodness but prefer to focus the attention on others; you do not see yourself as more special than others; you admit your imperfections.
○	**18. Prudence:** You are wisely cautious; you are planful and conscientious; you are careful to not take undue risks or do things you might later regret.
○	**19. Self-Regulation:** You are a very disciplined person; you manage your vices and bad habits; you stay calm and cool under pressure; you manage your impulses and emotions.
○	**20. Appreciation of Beauty & Excellence:** You notice the beauty and excellence around you; you are often awestruck by beauty, greatness, and/or the moral goodness you witness; you are often filled with wonder.
○	**21. Gratitude:** You regularly experience and express thankfulness; you don't take the good things that happen in your life for granted; you tend to feel blessed in many circumstances.
○	**22. Hope:** You are optimistic, expecting the best to happen; you believe in and work toward a positive future; you can think of many pathways to reach your goals.
○	**23. Humor:** You are playful; you love to make people smile and laugh; your sense of humor helps you connect closely to others; you brighten gloomy situations with fun and/or jokes.
○	**24. Spirituality:** Your life is infused with a sense of meaning and purpose; you feel a connection with something larger than yourself; your faith informs who you are and your place in the universe; you maintain a regular spiritual and/or religious practice.
○	**None of these characteristics is more essential to who I am than any of the others.** Choose this option if you feel the strengths are all equally essential to you, not because you think they should be equally essential.

Step 2

Review the strengths you checked. Do any of these strengths stand out as more important to who you are than the others? If so, put a second check next to those strengths. These are your signature strengths.

There is no exact number of signature strengths that you should have. The average number of signature strengths in studies with this test is about five or six. Pay close attention to those strengths that you gave two check-marks. These might be the character strengths that are most essential to who you are, easiest for you to use, and most energizing. If you checked off far more than five strengths, then go through it again and whittle the list down to the five that best capture who you are. If you found you did not check any strengths or only a couple, you might ask for someone close to you (such as a parent, friend, or counselor) to review the list and select the five strengths they see as strongest in you.[199]

Appendix C:

The Positive Judaism Passover Seder

The Passover seder is the single most observed Jewish ceremony each year. Now that you have learned the theories of well-being and the factors that influence happiness, challenge yourself to create a Positive Judaism Passover seder. A Passover gathering has the potential to incorporate PERMA, character strengths, and broaden-and-build practices to make any seder a complete experience of well-being and happiness. Here are some examples that you can use to incorporate the ten Jewish happiness virtues into a seder.

Gratitude: Welcome, Candle-Lighting, Opening Prayers

We welcome you to this seder. As we kindle these festival lights, we are grateful to be here with each other, sharing our lives together, humbly mindful of the gift of light and life. Rabbi Nachman of Breslov taught, "Gratitude rejoices with her sister joy and is always ready to light a candle and have a party. Gratitude doesn't much like the old cronies of boredom, despair, and taking life for granted."

Resilience: First Cup of Wine—*Kadeish*

We lift this cup of wine in honor of the Israelites who suffered under the yoke of slavery and for demonstrating resilience in the face of bondage. Resilience is the ability to remain active, energetic, focused, and flexible no matter what life presents. The inspiration for resilience is found in the words of Zechariah, "Not by might, not by power, but by My spirit."[200]

Optimism: It Would Have Been Enough! *Dayeinu!*

Dayeinu is a song of freedom and calls us to have hope and optimism in our lives and dream of a future where every living thing is treated with compassion, generosity, and love. The Psalmist writes, "And I shall always hope, and I shall add to all of Your praises."[201]

Perseverance: The Middle Matzah (*Afikoman*)—*Yachatz*

We set aside a broken piece of matzah that will become the *afikoman* to teach the value of perseverance, knowing that what seems broken may be repaired. The broken matzah honors the perseverance of the Israelites and their ability to persist in the face of great hardship and challenge. The fifteenth-century Spanish rabbi Isaac ben Moses Arama, also known as the Akeidat Yitzchak, taught, "Personal effort and perseverance contribute the major part to eventual success. In fact, any negligence or laziness is rated as sinful when circumstances seem to have called for exertion of the self."

Loving-Kindness: The Story of Matzah—*Maggid*

This is the bread of affliction that our ancestors ate on their journey to freedom. Let us show unwavering love and kindness to all who are hungry and enslaved today. We are all called in every generation to remember the Exodus "as if we were still slaves in Egypt," as when the Eternal passes in front of Moses and proclaims, "God, compassionate and gracious, slow to anger, abounding in love and kindness."[202]

Wisdom: The Four Children—*Arbaah Vanim*

The seder tradition speaks of four children: the wise, the wicked, the simple, and the one who does not know to ask. As guides to our children and to the next generation, we hope to instill a love of learning and a mind-set of growth. As it is written, "My child, do not forget my teaching, but let your mind retain these commandments; for it will bestow on you length of days, years of life and well-being."[203]

Courage: The Hillel Sandwich—*Motzi/Matzah/Maror/Charoset*—*Koreich*

The combination of the matzah, *maror*, and *charoset* teach us that life can be dry, sweet, and sometimes bitter. Yet when we rise to our challenges with courage, we can accomplish great things. "Ben Zoma taught: Who is courageous? Those who conquer their evil impulse. As it is written: 'Those who are slow to anger are better than the mighty, and those who rule over their spirit better than those who conquer a city.'"204

Forgiveness: The Passover Seder Meal—*Shulchan Oreich*

Mealtime is the perfect opportunity to express forgiveness to someone at this table as we share in the festive meal together and engage in positive conversations that enhance our seder. As the Torah teaches, "You shall love your neighbor as yourself."205

Justice: Finding the *Afikoman—Tzafun*

Searching for the hidden *afikoman* is a highlight for a child's seder experience and, when done fairly, can be one of the most memorable moments of the seder. The Proverbs teach, "For learning wisdom and discipline; for understanding words of discernment; for acquiring the discipline for success, righteousness, justice, and equity; for endowing the simple with shrewdness, the young with knowledge and foresight. The wise man, hearing them, will gain more wisdom; the discerning man will learn to be adroit."206

Spirituality: Open the Door for Elijah, Farewell—*Nirtzah*

As our Passover journey comes to an end, we open the door for the prophet Elijah, who symbolizes hope for a better world for all people. Having faith in a higher purpose and expressing connection and interest to the unknowable and unseen is a positive strength. With a final gesture of positivity, we express gratitude for those who prepared the seder meal, the seder leader(s), the hosts, the guests, and the Eternal One.

Acknowledgments

This is an important moment in history, and many within the Jewish community are thinking about how Jewish living pairs with human advancement. Jewish leaders are seeking ways to take the knowledge of modern science of the brain and the body and find ways to use that evidence to elevate the lives of people at camps, schools, community centers, and synagogues. There are many brilliant minds that have been imagining new ways for Judaism to thrive in the twenty-first century, and I hope this book helps push our work forward.

I would like to thank the presenters at the first Positive Judaism Summits. You are the intellectual partners of this positive vision for Jewish life in the twenty-first century. You are the thought leaders of the Jewish future, and I am honored to know you: Rabbi Uri Allen, Christina Broussard, Dr. David Bryfman, Cantor Adina Frydman, Rabbi Matthew Gewitz, Rabbi Elisa Goldberg, Dr. Jeff Kress, Tali Kurt-Galai, Lisa Litman, Anna Marx, Rabbi Michael Mellen, Rabbi Geoff Mittelman, Rabbi Avi Orlow, Chesney Polis, Dr. Bill Robinson, Rabbi Jessica Rosenberg, Dr. Evie Rotstein, Aaron Selkow, Rabbi Michelle Shapiro Abraham, Rabbi Rebecca Sirbu, Rabbi Mike Uram, Rabbi Phil Warmflash, and Rabbi Deborah Waxman.

Thank you to Dr. Martin Seligman and my fellow participants at the Imagination Institute retreat in the summer of 2017. The purpose of the gathering was to explore spiritual imagination, and many of the core ideas in this book emerged from our discussions. I am indebted each of you: Dr. Roy Baumeister, Bill Bradley, Betty Sue Flowers, James Hovey, Rev. Serene Jones, Dr. Scott Barry Kaufman, Chicaco Matsumoto, Naomi Shihab Nye, Dr. Arthur Schwartz, Krista Tippett, Stuart Warren, and David Yaden.

Thank you to my mentors who nourished the ideas of Positive Judaism in your special and unique ways over the years: Rabbi Billy Dreskin, Rabbi David Gelfand, Rabbi Arthur Gross-Schaefer, Rabbi Steven Leder, Rabbi Mark Miller *z"l*, Rabbi Jonathan Stein, and Rhoda Weisman. And thank you to the listeners of the *Positive Judaism* podcast and the *Positive Judaism* blog who write me with your reactions to the entries and the episodes. I cherish our conversations.

Thank you to the members of my home congregation, Tamid: The Downtown Synagogue in New York City. We have been engaged with these ideas since we started our community in 2011. Thank you for experimenting with aspects of Positive Judaism and for encouraging me to write this book, which I did in the summer of 2018 in Boulder, Colorado. I chose this city because it ranks as one the best in the United States for well-being and happiness.

Each day, when I sat down to write, I put three small rocks on my table, each representing a different audience to whom this book is written. One rock was for my students and my congregants who are seeking to have the most positive impact in the world and to live full and meaningful lives. The second was for my faith colleagues who are working in religious settings, eager to make a positive impact on the communities, schools, and organizations they serve. And the third was for my professional colleagues in the mental health field who are steeped in the science of well-being and positive psychology. Thank you for keeping me company over those long hours of writing and rewriting.

Thank you to the librarians and staff at the University of Colorado Norlin Library for helping me access databases and information. A heartfelt thanks to Elizabeth Hyde for your advice and guidance on how to best interpret the positive psychology literature. Thank you to Lilach Bonani, Marnie Braverman, Christina Broussard, and Tobin and Trudy Duisenberg for commenting on early drafts. And a special thanks to Jenna and Ken Richer for hosting me in Colorado.

Thank you to my friend and book agent, Richard Curtis. Early in my career, Richard and I spent many Shabbat mornings together at minyan and Torah study, and I have always respected Richard's keen mind. Thank you for believing in Positive Judaism and for being my advocate, guide, and ambassador.

With tremendous respect, gratitude, and admiration, thank you David Behrman and Dena Neusner at Behrman House for your literary partnership. In sum, you believed that a book about Positive Judaism could help people improve their lives, and that confidence carried me as we built and rebuilt the framework of this book. Thank you for all the wise counsel and especially for asking Kathy Bloomfield to edit this book. Kathy and I clicked immediately, and her invisible fingerprints are on every page of this book; thank you, Kathy.

And most importantly, I want to thank my parents, my children, and my extended family, with love and admiration: Susan, David, Emmett, Adrian, Robin, Adam, Noah, Eli, Simon, Donna, Rhoda, Julia, Beverly, Sheri, Marshall, Jason, Glaucia, and Marc.

Notes

Introduction: A New Vision for Jewish Life in the Twenty-First Century

1 Ellie Polack, "New Cigna Study Reveals Loneliness at Epidemic Levels in America," Cigna, May 1, 2018, www.cigna.com/newsroom/news-releases/2018/new-cigna-study-reveals-loneliness-at-epidemic-levels-in-america.

2 Pew Research Center: Religion & Public Life, "Religious Landscape Study: Attendance at Religious Services," Pew Research Center, www.pewforum.org/religious-landscape-study/attendance-at-religious-services.

3 David Shimer, "Yale's Most Popular Class Ever: Happiness," *New York Times*, January 26, 2018, www.nytimes.com/2018/01/26/nyregion/at-yale-class-on-happiness-draws-huge-crowd-laurie-santos.html.

4 Centre for Bhutan Studies & GNH Research, *A Compass towards a Just and Harmonious Society: 2015 GNH Report* (Thimphu, Butan: Centre for Bhutan Studies & GNH Research, 2016), www.grossnationalhappiness.com/wp-content/uploads/2017/01/Final-GNH-Report-jp-21.3.17-ilovepdf-compressed.pdf.

5 "The General Assembly of the United Nations, resolution 66/281 of 12 July 2012, proclaimed 20 March the International Day of Happiness," United Nations, www.un.org/en/events/happinessday.

Part One: Ancient Wisdom, Modern Science

6 Tom Rath and Jim Harter, *Wellbeing: The Five Essential Elements* (New York: Gallup Press, 2014).

Chapter 1: The Science of Well-Being and Happiness

7 Babylonian Talmud, *Shabbat* 31a.

8 Aristotle, *The Nicomachean Ethics: Oxford World Classics* (Oxford: Oxford University Press, 2009), section 21; 1095a 15–22.

9 Genesis 28:10–17, in *JPS Hebrew-English Tanakh: The Traditional Hebrew Text and the New JPS Translation*, 2nd ed. (Philadelphia: Jewish Publication Society, 1999), 56.

10 Psalm 128:2.

11 Tom Rath and Jim Harter, *Wellbeing: The Five Essential Elements* (New York: Gallup Press, 2014), 5.

12 Rath and Harter, *Wellbeing*, 153–54.

13 Martin E. P. Seligman, *Flourish: A Visionary New Understanding of Happiness and Well-Being* (New York: Free Press, 2011), 15.

14 Sonja Lyubomirsky, *The How of Happiness: A New Approach to Getting the Life You Want* (New York: Penguin, 2007), 228–39.

15 C. G. Ellison, and J. S. Levin, "The Religion-Health Connection: Evidence, Theory, and Future Directions," *Health Education and Behaviour* 25 (December 1998): 700–20.

16 Ellison and Levin, "The Religion-Health Connection."

17 Ellison and Levin, "The Religion-Health Connection."

18 Lea Waters, *The Strength Switch: How the New Science of Strength-Based Parenting Can Help Your Child and Your Teen to Flourish* (New York: Avery, 2017).

19 "VIA Classifications of Character Strengths and Virtues," VIA Institute on Character, 2018, www.viacharacter.org/www/Portals/0/Icons%20Classification%20Adult2_1.pdf.

20 Waters, *The Strength Switch*, 9.

21 Darren Levine, "Positive Judaism: A First Glance for Clergy and Jewish Educators," *CCAR Journal*, Summer 2017.

22 Babylonian Talmud, *Avodah Zarah* 18:8.

23 Pirkei Avot 6:6.

24 Pirkei Avot 2:1; Maimonides, *Mishneh Torah, Hilchot Dei'ot* 1:3–4.

25 Barbara L. Fredrickson, *Positivity: Top-Notch Research Reveals the Upward Spiral That Will Change Your Life* (New York: Three Rivers Press, 2009), 21.

26 Barbara L. Fredrickson, "The Broaden-and-Build Theory of Positive Emotions," *Philosophical Transactions of the Royal Society Biological Sciences* 359, no. 1449 (2004): 1367–78.

27 Shelly L. Gable et al., "What Do You Do When Things Go Right? The Intrapersonal and Interpersonal Benefits of Sharing Positive Events," *Journal of Personality and Social Psychology* 87, no. 2 (2004): 228–45.

28 Sarah D. Pressman and Sheldon Cohen, "Does Positive Affect Influence Health?," *Psychological Bulletin* 131, no. 6 (2005): 925–71.

29 Pirkei Avot 4:2.

30 Maimonides, *Mishneh Torah, Hilchot T'shuvah* 5:2.

31 Lyubomirsky, *The How of Happiness*.

32 Babylonian Talmud, *Bava Kama* 3b.

33 Lyubomirsky, *The How of Happiness*, 22–23.

Chapter 2: Positive Judaism: Principles, Practices, and Virtues

34 Alvin Fine, in *Rabbi's Manual of the Central Conference of American Rabbis*, ed. David Polish and W. Gunther Plaut (New York: CCAR Press, 1988), 138–40.

35 Job 9:25, in *JPS Hebrew-English Tanakh: The Traditional Hebrew Text and the New JPS Translation*, 2nd ed. (Philadelphia: Jewish Publication Society, 1999), 1671.

36 Fine, in *Rabbi's Manual of the Central Conference of American Rabbis*.

37 Leviticus 19:18.

38 Babylonian Talmud, *Shabbat* 31a.

39 Maimonides, *Mishneh Torah, Hilchot Dei'ot* 4:1.

Chapter 3: Relationships: Marriage, Family, and Parenting

40 Tom Rath and Jim Harter, *Wellbeing: The Five Essential Elements* (New York: Gallup Press, 2014).

41 Leviticus 19:18.

42 Shelly L. Gable et al., "What Do You Do When Things Go Right?," *Journal of Personality and Social Psychology* 87, no. 2 (2004): 228–45.

43 John Gottman and Nan Silver, *What Makes Love Last? How to Build Trust and Avoid Betrayal* (New York: Simon and Schuster, 2012), 210–12.

44 Martin Buber, *I and Thou*, trans. Walter Kaufman (New York: Scribner, 1970), 130.

45 Emanuel Levinas, *Totality and Infinity: An Essay on Exteriority* (New York: Springer Science & Business Media, 1961), 262.

46 Proverbs 31:10, in *JPS Hebrew-English Tanakh: The Traditional Hebrew Text and the New JPS Translation*, 2nd ed. (Philadelphia: Jewish Publication Society, 1999), 1654.

47 Ed Diener and Eunkook M. Suh, eds., *Culture and Subjective Well-Being* (Cambridge, MA: MIT Press, 2003).

48 Genesis 2:18, in *JPS Hebrew English Tanakh*, 4.

49 John Gottman and Nan Silver, *What Makes Love Last? How to Build Trust and Avoid Betrayal* (New York: Simon & Schuster, 2012), 237.

50 The author's modern English translation of the seventh or the final blessing in the "*sheva b'rachot*," the seven Jewish wedding blessings.

51 Genesis 1:3, in *JPS Hebrew-English Tanakh*, 1.

52 Babylonian Talmud, *Sotah* 3b.

53 Psalm 34:15, in *JPS Hebrew-English Tanakh*, 1450.

54 S. Katherine Nelson, Kostadin Kushlev, and Sonja Lyubomirsky, "The Pains and Pleasures of Parenting: When, Why, and How Is Parenthood Associated with More or Less Well-Being?," *Psychological Bulletin* 140, no. 3 (2014): 846–95.

55 Laura L. Carstensen, Monisha Pasupathi, Ulrich Mayr, and John Nesselroade, "Emotional Experience in Everyday Life across the Adult Life Span," *Journal of Personality and Social Psychology* 79 (October 2000): 644–55.

56 Hara Estroff Marano, "The Art of Resilience," *Psychology Today*, May 1, 2003, www.psychologytoday.com/us/articles/200305/the-art-resilience.

57 Barbara Fredrickson, *LOVE 2.0: Finding Happiness and Health in Moments of Connection* (New York: Hudson Street Press, 2013), 78.

58 Babylonian Talmud, *Kiddushin* 30b.

59 Lea Waters, *The Strength Switch: How the New Science of Strength-Based Parenting Can Help Your Child and Your Teen to Flourish* (New York: Avery, 2017), 7.

60 For the complete character strength inventory, see "VIA Classifications of Character Strengths and Virtues," VIA Institute on Character, 2018, www.viacharacter.org/www/Portals/0/Icons%20Classification%20Adult2_1.pdf.

61 Waters, *The Strength Switch*.

62 Proverbs 2:1–5, in *JPS Hebrew-English Tanakh*, 1601.

Chapter 4: Health: Physical and Mental Well-Being

63 Maimonides, *Mishneh Torah, Hilchot Dei'ot* 4:1.

64 Tom Rath and Jim Harter, *Wellbeing: The Five Essential Elements* (New York: Gallup Press, 2014), 88.

65 Rabbi Samson Raphael Hirsch commentary on Horeb, chapter 62, section 428.

66 Maimonides, *Mishneh Torah, Hilchot Dei'ot* 4:1.

67 Genesis 1:27.

68 *Toldot HaChafetz Chayim*, quoted in Yechezkel Ishayek, *Chayim Beriyim Kehalacha* (B'nai Brak, 2007), 29.

69 Maimonides, *Mishneh Torah, Hilchot Dei'ot* 4:1.

70 *Leviticus Rabbah* 34:3.

71 Barbara L. Fredrickson et al., "What Good Are Positive Emotions in Crises? A Prospective Study of Resilience and Emotions Following the Terrorist Attacks on the United States on September 11th, 2001," *Journal of Personality and Social Psychology* 84, no. 2 (February 2003): 365–76.

72 Martin E. P. Seligman, *Learned Optimism: How to Change Your Mind and Your Life* (New York: Vintage Books, 2006).

73 L. Aspinwall and S. Brunhart, "Distinguishing Optimism from Denial: Optimistic Benefits Predict Attention to Health Threats," *Personality and Social Psychology Bulletin* 22, no. 10 (1996): 993–1003.

74 Seligman, *Learned Optimism*.

75 Psalm 71:14, in *JPS Hebrew-English Tanakh: The Traditional Hebrew Text and the New JPS Translation*, 2nd ed. (Philadelphia: Jewish Publication Society, 1999), 1498.

76 Seligman, *Learned Optimism*.

77 Seligman, *Learned Optimism*.

78 *The Observer* (London), December 29, 1974, 14.

79 Lawrence Wright, *Thirteen Days in September: The Dramatic Struggle for Peace* (New York: Vintage Books, 2015).

80 Numbers 13:32–33, in *JPS Hebrew-English Tanakh*, 313.

81 Numbers 14:7–9, in *JPS Hebrew-English Tanakh*, 313.

82 Kenneth I. Pargament and Annette Mahoney, "Spirituality: The Search for the Sacred," in *The Oxford Handbook of Positive Psychology*, 2nd ed., ed. Shane J. Lopez and C. R. Snyder (Oxford: Oxford University Press, 2011), 646–59.

83 Daniel Mochon, Michael I. Norton, and Dan Ariely, "Getting Off the Hedonic Treadmill, One Step at a Time: The Impact of Regular Religious Practice and Exercise on Well-Being," *Journal of Economic Psychology* 29 (November 2008): 632–42.

84 N. M. Lambert et al., "Can Prayer Increase Gratitude?," *Psychology of Religion and Spirituality* 1, no. 3 (2009): 139–49.

85 Wisdom of Solomon 7:7, www.kingjamesbibleonline.org/Wisdom-of-Solomon-7-7.

Chapter 5: Community: Bringing People Together

86 Tom Rath and Jim Harter, *Wellbeing: The Five Essential Elements* (New York: Gallup Press, 2014), 103.

87 Ellie Polack, "New Cigna Study Reveals Loneliness at Epidemic Levels in America," Cigna, May 1, 2018, www.cigna.com/newsroom/news-releases/2018/new-cigna-study-reveals-loneliness-at-epidemic-levels-in-america.

88 Anne Berthold and Willibald Ruch, "Satisfaction with Life and Character Strengths of Non-religious and Religious People: It's Practicing One's Religion That Makes the Difference," *Frontiers in Psychology* 5 (August 2014): article 876.

89 Rob Stein, "Happiness Can Spread Among People Like a Contagion, Study Indicates," *Washington Post*, December 5, 2008.

90 Doug Oman and Dwayne Reed, "Religion and Mortality among the Community-Dwelling Elderly," *American Journal of Public Health* 88 (November 1998): 1469–75.

91 Robert A. Emmons, *The Psychology of Ultimate Concerns: Motivation and Spirituality in Personality* (New York: Guilford Press, 2003).

92 Olga Stavrova, Detlef Fetchenhauer, and Thomas Schlösser, "Why Are Religious People Happy? The Effect of the Social Norm of Religiosity across Countries," *Social Science Research* 42, no. 1 (January 2013): 90–105.

93 Babylonian Talmud, *Sh'vuot* 39a.

94 Pirkei Avot 1:2.

95 Psalm 23:6.

96 Exodus 34:6.

97 Pirkei Avot 2:8.

Chapter 6: Work: Make Your Calling Your Career

98 Babylonian Talmud, *Sanhedrin* 24b.

99 Tom Rath and Jim Harter, *Wellbeing: The Five Essential Elements* (New York: Gallup Press, 2014), 28.

100 Harris Interactive, "Stress in the Workplace: American Psychological Association Harris Interactive, Survey Summary," American Psychological Association, March 2011, https://www.apa.org/news/press/releases/phwa-survey-summary.pdf.

101 Exodus 20:12, in *JPS Hebrew-English Tanakh: The Traditional Hebrew Text and the New JPS Translation*, 2nd ed. (Philadelphia: Jewish Publication Society, 1999), 158.

102 John H. Pryor et al., *The American Freshman: National Norms Fall 2010* (Los Angeles: Higher Education Research Institute, UCLA, 2010).

103 Harris Interactive, "Stress in the Workplace."

104 Roy J. deCarvalho, "Maslow, Abraham Harold," *American National Biography Online*, 2000, https://doi.org/10.1093/anb/9780198606697.article.1400858.

105 Parker Palmer, *Let Your Life Speak: Listening to the Voice of Vocation* (San Francisco: Jossey-Bass, 2000).

106 Babylonian Talmud, *Ta'anit* 23a.

107 Proverbs 1:2–3, in *JPS Hebrew-English Tanakh*, 1599.

108 Proverbs 1:5.

109 Proverbs 19:8, in *JPS Hebrew-English Tanakh*, 1631.

Chapter 7: Money: Earn It Well, Spend It Wisely

110 *Sefer HaKuzari*, 3:11.

111 Tom Rath and Jim Harter, *Wellbeing: The Five Essential Elements* (New York: Gallup Press, 2014).

112 Lara B. Aknin, Michael I. Norton, and Elizabeth W. Dunn, "From Wealth to Well-Being? Money Matters, but Less Than People Think," *Journal of Positive Psychology* 4, no. 6 (November 2009): 523–27.

113 Ecclesiastes 5:9, in *JPS Hebrew-English Tanakh: The Traditional Hebrew Text and the New JPS Translation*, 2nd ed. (Philadelphia: Jewish Publication Society, 1999), 1772.

114 Daniel Kahneman and Angus Deaton, "High Income Improves Evaluation of Life but Not Emotional Well-Being," *Proceedings of the National Academy of Sciences of the United States of America* 107, no. 38 (September 2010): 16489–93.

115 Dylan M. Smith, Kenneth M. Langa, and Mohammed U. Kabeto, "Health, Wealth, and Happiness: Financial Resources Buffer Subjective Well Being after the Onset of a Disability," *Psychological Science* 16 (September 2005): 663–66.

116 Shlomo ibn Gabirol, *Mivchar Hapeninim* (Jerusalem: Vagshal, 1995), 155, 161.

117 Elizabeth W. Dunn, Lara B. Aknin, and Michael I. Norton, "Spending Money on Others Promotes Happiness," *Science* 319 (March 2008): 1687–88.

118 Solomon ibn Gabirol, *Pearls of Wisdom* (Jerusalem: Vagshal, 1995), 155, 161.

119 Sonja Lyubomirsky. *The Myths of Happiness: What Should Make You Happy, but Doesn't, What Shouldn't Make You Happy, but Does* (New York: Penguin Press, 2013), 175.

120 Lara B. Aknin, Elizabeth Dunn, and Michael I. Norton, "Prosocial Spending and Happiness: Using Money to Benefit Others Pays Off," *Current Directions in Psychological Science* 23, no. 1 (2014): 41–47.

121 Lara B. Aknin et al., "Prosocial Spending and Well-Being: Cross-Cultural Evidence for a Psychological Universal," *Journal of Personality and Social Psychology* 104, no. 4 (2013): 635–652.

122 Elizabeth Dunn and Michael Norton, *Happy Money: The Science of Happier Spending* (New York: Simon & Schuster, 2014), 113.

123 Deuteronomy 15:7–8, in *JPS Hebrew English Tanakh*, 408.

124 George Robinson, "Tzedakah in the Jewish Tradition," My Jewish Learning, www.myjewishlearning.com/article/tzedakah-in-the-jewish-tradition, excerpted from George Robinson, *Essential Judaism* (New York: Simon and Schuster, 2008).

125 *Numbers Rabbah* 5:2.

Chapter 8: When Relationships Fall Apart: Broken Bonds, Separation, and Divorce

126 Ed Diener and Eunkook M. Suh, eds., *Culture and Subjective Well-Being* (Cambridge MA: MIT Press, 2003).

127 Paul R. Amato, "Research on Divorce: Continuing Developments and New Trends," *Journal of Marriage and the Family* 72 (2010): 650–66.

128 R. J. Fazio, "Growth Consulting: Practical Methods of Facilitating Growth through Loss and Adversity," *Journal of Clinical Psychology* 65 (May 2009): 532–43.

129 Martin E. P. Seligman et al., *The Optimistic Child: A Proven Program to Safeguard Children against Depression and Build Lifelong Resilience* (New York: Houghton Mifflin, 2007).

130 Jennifer E. Lansford, "Parental Divorce and Children's Adjustment," *Perspectives on Psychological Science* 4, no. 2 (2009): 140–52.

131 J. Holt-Lunstad, T. B. Smith, and J. B. Layton, "Social Relationships and Mortality Risk: A Meta-Analytic Review," *Public Library of Science Medicine* 7 (2010): 7.

132 Jerusalem Talmud, *Ketubot* 11:3.

133 Maimonides, *Mishneh Torah, Hilchot T'shuvah* 2:10

134 M. E. McCullough and C. V. Witvliet, "The Psychology of Forgiveness," in *The Oxford Handbook of Positive Psychology*, 2nd ed., ed. Shane J. Lopez and C. R. Snyder (Oxford: Oxford University Press, 2011), 446–58.

135 "Hannah Arendt Quotes," BrainyQuote, BrainyMedia, 2019, www.brainyquote.com/quotes/hannah_arendt_100489.

136 Genesis 45:5,7–8, in *JPS Hebrew-English Tanakh: The Traditional Hebrew Text and the New JPS Translation*, 2nd ed. (Philadelphia: Jewish Publication Society, 1999), 98.

137 Mary Ann Lamanna, Agnes Riedmann, and Susan D. Stewart, *Marriages, Families, and Relationships: Making Choices in a Diverse Society* (Boston: Cengage Learning Publishers, 2015), 364.

138 Harey Mocheni prayer on Yom Kippur, the holiest day on the Jewish calendar. See any traditional High Holiday prayer book for the Yom Kippur service.

139 See any traditional High Holiday prayer book for the evening Yom Kippur ceremony.

Chapter 9: When Illness Comes: Coping with Pain and Sickness

140 Richard G. Tedeschi and Lawrence G. Calhoun, "Posttraumatic Growth: Conceptual Foundations and Empirical Evidence," *Psychological Inquiry* 15, no. 1 (2004): 1–18.

141 David Gutierrez, "More Proof That Prayer Works? Religious Patients Found to Be Healthier Than Others," *Natural News*, August 2015, www.naturalnews. com/050930_prayer_overcoming_cancer_spirituality.html.

142 Babylonian Talmud, *B'rachot* 5b.

143 *Genesis Rabbah* 8:13.

144 Jon Kabat-Zinn, *Full Catastrophe Living: Using the Wisdom of Your Body and Mind to Face Stress, Pain and Illness* (New York: Bantam Books, 2013).

145 R. J. Davidson et al., "Alterations in Brain and Immune Function Produced by Mindfulness Meditation," *Psychosomatic Medicine* 65, no. 4 (July–August 2003): 564–70.

146 W. P. Smith, W. C. Compton, and W. B. West, "Meditation as an Adjunct to a Happiness Enhancement Program," *Journal of Clinical Psychology* 51, no. 2 (March 1995): 269–73.

147 Genesis 22:1.

148 Genesis 37:13.

149 Exodus 3:4.

150 Mihaly Csikszentmihalyi, *Flow: The Psychology of Optimal Experience* (New York: Harper Perennial, 1990). Flow is defined as "optimal experience" where people typically experience deep enjoyment, creativity, and a total involvement with life.

151 The opposite of courage is fear. This comes from Chris Peterson's "Unfinished Masterpiece," which Dr. Seligman calls "the Peterson pathologies." These qualities are the opposite of the virtues and exist in the absence of the positive quality. In positive psychology and our method, similar to Noah in this example, rather than treat the problem by fixing the deficiency, we work on fostering the positive virtue.

152 "Viktor E. Frankl Quotes," Goodreads, www.goodreads.com/author/ quotes/2782.Viktor_E_Frankl.

153 *Avot d'Rabbi Natan* 39:1.

Chapter 10: Alone in the World: Facing Loneliness and Isolation

154 Pirkei Avot 1:6.

155 Ellie Polack, "New Cigna Study Reveals Loneliness at Epidemic Levels in America," Cigna, May 2018, www.cigna.com/newsroom/news-releases/2018/new-cigna-study-reveals-loneliness-at-epidemic-levels-in-america.

156 Psalm 25:16–17.

157 "Bernard Lawrence Madoff is an American former market maker, investment advisor, financier, fraudster, and convicted felon, who is currently serving a federal prison sentence for offenses related to a massive Ponzi scheme. "Bernard Madoff," Wikipedia, accessed February 1, 2019, www.en.wikipedia.org/w/index.php?title=Bernard_Madoff&oldid=879752681.

158 Marc Katz, *The Heart of Loneliness: How Jewish Wisdom Can Help You Cope and Find Comfort* (Nashville, TN: Jewish Lights, 2016).

159 Elizabeth M. Perse and Alan M. Rubin, "Chronic Loneliness and Television Use," *Journal of Broadcasting and Electronic Media* 34, no. 1 (January 1990): 37–53.

160 Emily Caldwell, "Loneliness, Like Chronic Stress, Taxes the Immune System," *Research and Innovation Communications*, Ohio State University, January 2013.

161 J. Holt-Lunstad, T. B. Smith, and J. B. Layton, "Social Relationships and Mortality Risk: A Meta-Analytic Review," *Public Library of Science Medicine* 7 (2010): 4016.

162 Holt-Lunstad, Smith, and Layton, "Social Relationships and Mortality Risk."

163 Rhitu Chatterjee, "Americans Are a Lonely Lot, and Young People Bear the Heaviest Burden," *Shots: Health News from NPR*, NPR, May 1, 2018, www.npr.org/sections/health-shots/2018/05/01/606588504/americans-are-a-lonely-lot-and-young-people-bear-the-heaviest-burdenCigna Study.

164 *Genesis Rabbah* 17:4.

165 Genesis 3:9, in *JPS Hebrew-English Tanakh: The Traditional Hebrew Text and the New JPS Translation*, 2nd ed. (Philadelphia: Jewish Publication Society, 1999), 5.

166 Psalm 91:15, in *JPS Hebrew-English Tanakh*, 1528.

167 *Exodus Rabbah* 2:5.

168 *Oxford English Dictionary*, https://en.oxforddictionaries.com.

169 Peter Harrison, *The Territories of Science and Religion* (Chicago: University of Chicago Press, 2015).

170 Bahya Ben Joseph (Ibn Pakuda), *The Book of Direction to the Duties of the Heart*, trans. Menaham Mansoor (London: Routledge & Kegan Paul), 109.

171 Sonja Lyubomirsky, *The How of Happiness: A New Approach to Getting the Life You Want* (New York: Penguin, 2007), 232.

Chapter 11: When the Work Is Not Working: Job Loss and Forced Career Change

172 "Suicide Statistics," 2017, American Foundation for Suicide Prevention, www.afsp.org/about-suicide/suicide-statistics.

173 Al Siebert, *The Survivor Personality: Why Some People are Stronger, Smarter, and More Skillfull at Handling Life's Difficulties . . . and How You Can Be, Too* (New York: TarcherPerigee, 1996).

174 Stephanie Spera, Eric Buhrfiend, and James Pennebaker, "Expressive Writing and Coping with Job Loss," *Academy of Management Journal* 37, no. 3 (June 1994): 722–33, www.journals.aom.org/doi/abs/10.5465/256708?journalCode=amj.

175 Robert Emmons and Michael McCullough, *The Psychology of Gratitude* (New York: Oxford University Press, 2004).

176 Babylonian Talmud, *Ta'anit* 21a.

177 *P'sikta d'Rav Kahana* 12:9.

178 Exodus 14:13–15, in *JPS Hebrew-English Tanakh: The Traditional Hebrew Text and the New JPS Translation*, 2nd ed. (Philadelphia: Jewish Publication Society, 1999), 142.

179 Victor Frankl, *Man's Search for Meaning* (Boston: Beacon Press, 2014), 165.

180 Menachem Mendel Schneerson, *Likutei Sichot*, vol. 10 (New York: Kehot Publication Society, 2002), 25.

181 J. A. Piliavin, "Doing Well by Doing Good: Benefits for the Benefactor," in *Flourishing: Positive Psychology and the Life Well Lived*, ed. Corey L. M. Keyes and Jonathan Haidt (Washington, DC: American Psychological Association, 2003), 227–47.

182 Leon Uris, *QB VII* (New York: Doubleday, 1970)

183 Leviticus 23:22.

Chapter 12: Upside Down: Dealing with Financial Trouble

184 Elie Weisel, *Open Heart*, trans. Marion Weisel (New York: Knopf, 2012), 72.

185 Isaac ben Moses Arama, *Akeidat Yitzchak* 25:16.

186 Sharon Salzberg, *Lovingkindness: The Revolutionary Art of Happiness* (Boston: Shambala, 1995).

187 National Center for Complementary and Integrative Health, "Meditation," National Institutes of Health, September 24, 2017, www.nccih.nih.gov/health/meditation.

188 Ryan M. Niemiec, *Mindfulness and Character Strengths: A Practical Guide to Flourishing* (Boston: Hogrefe, 2014), 18.

189 Bachya ben Joseph ibn Pakuda and Daniel Haberman, *Chovot Halevavot / Duties of the Heart* (Nanuet, NY: Feldheim, 1996).

190 Nancy Flam, "The Jewish Way of Healing," *Reform Jewish Magazine*, Summer 1994.

191 From the weekday Amidah prayer.

192 From the Shabbat morning Shacharit Amidah.

193 Psalms 31:6 and 3:6–7.

194 Psalm 145:18.

195 Psalm 118:24.

Part Four: The Journey Forward: The Future of Positive Judaism

196 Deuteronomy 11:19.

197 Proverbs 3:2, in *JPS Hebrew-English Tanakh: The Traditional Hebrew Text and the New JPS Translation*, 2nd ed. (Philadelphia: Jewish Publication Society, 1999), 1602.

Appendixes

198 Adapted from Julie Butler and Margaret L. Kern, "The PERMA-Profiler: A Brief Multidimensional Measure of Flourishing," *International Journal of Wellbeing* 6, no. 3 (2016): 1–48.

199 Ryan M. Niemic. *The Power of Character Strengths: Appreciate and Ignite Your Positive Personality* (Cincinnati: VIA Institute on Character, 2019).

200 Zechariah 4:6, in *JPS Hebrew-English Tanakh: The Traditional Hebrew Text and the New JPS Translation*, 2nd ed. (Philadelphia: Jewish Publication Society, 1999), 1387.

201 Psalm 71:14.

202 Exodus 34:6.

203 Proverbs 3:1–2, in *JPS Hebrew-English Tanakh*, 1602.

204 Pirkei Avot 4:1.

205 Leviticus 19:18.

206 Proverbs 1:2–5, in *JPS Hebrew-English Tanakh*, 1599.

Index of Jewish Happiness Virtues and Jewish Well-Being Practices

Join Positive Judaism Online
www.positive-judaism.org

Resources for educators and clergy
Positive Judaism podcast
Study guides for groups and individuals
Book discussion guide
Join the annual Positive Judaism Summit

The author is grateful for the following text permissions:

Reproduced from *JPS Hebrew-English Tanakh: The Traditional Hebrew Text and the New JPS Translation*, 2nd ed, by permission of the University of Nebraska Press. Copyright 1999 by The Jewish Publication Society, Philadelphia.

VIA Classification of Character Strengths and Virtues and VIA Signature Strengths Survey copyright © 2004-2020 VIA Institute on Character. Used with permission. All rights reserved. www.viacharacter.org

"Birth is a Beginning" by Alvin Fine from *Rabbi's Manual* © 1988 by Central Conference of American Rabbis. Used by permission of the Central Conference of American Rabbis. All rights reserved.

PERMA Well-Being Profiler adapted with permission by Butler, J., & Kern, M. L. (2016). "The PERMA-Profiler: A Brief Multidimensional Measure of Flourishing," *International Journal of Wellbeing*, 6, 1-48. http://dx.doi.org/10.5502/ijw.v6i3.1